CHARLES BUKOWSKI Epic *Glottis*:

His Art & His Women (& me)

Henry Charles Bukowski was born in Andernach, Germany, on August 16, 1920. From age three until his death on March 9, 1994, Bukowski lived and wrote in Southern California. His many books of poetry and prose, most published by John Martin's Black Sparrow Press, have sold millions of copies throughout the world.

CHARLES BUKOWSKI Epic *Glottis*
His Art & His Women (& me)
by
Joan Jobe Smith

Foreword by Pamela Miller Wood

Poems & Essays by Fred Voss

SILVER BIRCH PRESS

Los Angeles, California, USA

ISBN-13: 978-0615702285

ISBN-10: 0615702287

FIRST EDITION, 2012

Email: silverbirchpress@yahoo.com
Web: silverbirchpress.com
Blog: http://silverbirchpress.wordpress.com

Cover Design: Joan Jobe Smith and Marilyn Johnson
Cover Photo: "Joanie Gentry @ The Playgirl Club, 1969" by Big Dave
Book Design: Silver Birch Press

Art by: Charles Bukowski, Henry Denander (www.henrydenander.com), David Hernandez, Marilyn Johnson, Billy Jones, Loren Kantor (woodcutting-fool.blogspot.com), Graziano Origa, Matt Sesow (www.sesow.com), David Scott, Joan Jobe Smith, (all USED BY PERMISSION).

Photo: "Charles Bukowski on Bench, New Orleans 1963" by Gypsy Lou Webb (Courtesy of Ann Menebroker), USED BY PERMISSION.

Additional Photos: Roni Braun, G. Freihalter, Linda King, Richard E. Lee, Gerard K. Love, Steve Lovsteen, Michael Pulley, Joan Jobe Smith, Dirk Velvet, Melanie Villines, Fred Voss, Annerose Schneider Watts (all USED BY PERMISSION).

ACKNOWLEDGMENTS

The author wishes to acknowledge the following anthologies and literary/online journals where many of these, essays, interviews, and poems have appeared over the years: *A Common Thread* (chance press), *AMBIT* (UK), *BEAT SCENE* (UK), *Beside the City of Angels* (World Parade Books), *Bukowski Boulevard* (Pearl Limited Editions), *Bukowski Review #1*, *Bukowski Symposium Newsletter* (Germany), *Chiron Review*, *Cultural Weekly*, *DAS IST ALLES: Charles Bukowski Recollected* (Pearl Editions), *Drinking with Bukowski* (Thunder Mouth Press), *How Dirty Girls Get Clean*, *Jehovah Jukebox* (Event Horizon), *Last Call* (Lummox Press), *Nerve Cowboy*, *OUTLAW BIBLE*, *Picking the Lock On the Door to Paradise* (Liquid Paper Press), *The Pow Wow Café* (The Poetry Business, UK), *PURR*, *Sequin Soul* (chance press), *Shakespeare N'A Jamais Fait Ca* (13eNote, Paris, France), *SURE*, *Teatime @ the Bouquet Morale* (w/Fred Voss, Liquid Paper Press) and *Wormwood Review*:68, 105, 117 & 133.

Fred Voss Acknowledgements: *Charles Bukowski Recollected: DAS IST ALLES*, Shakespeare N'a Jamais Fait Ca (13eNote, Paris, France), ART THAT ROARS with Mark Weber, Zerx Press, *Bukowski Review #1*, *Drinking with Bukowski* (Thunder's Mouth Press)

With Special Gratitude and Respect to the following editors and incomparable mentors for their art, personal encouragement and professional consideration during the past decades and recent months:

Martin Bax

Janet Fisher

Marilyn Johnson

Linda King

Leo J. Mailman

Ann Menebroker

Pamela Miller Wood

Anaïs Nin

David Scott

Jules Smith

Paul Tayyar

Melanie Villines

Fred Voss

and most of all:

HENRY CHARLES BUKOWSKI

and **MARVIN MALONE**

Joan Jobe Smith, 1975

TABLE OF CONTENTS

FOREWORD

By *Pamela Miller Wood*
Author of *CHARLES BUKOWSKI'S SCARLET*

I CAN'T THINK OF ANYONE BETTER QUALIFIED THAN JOAN JOBE SMITH to write about Charles Bukowski, his art, and his women. In 1973, while an undergrad at California State University at Long Beach, Joan's passion for English literature —poetry in particular —coupled with the stark absence of female expression in this arena, became her impetus to forge the first all-female poetry magazine simply titled *Pearl*.

During this time, Joan became aware of Charles Bukowski and his then-girlfriend, Linda King. By now, Bukowski had read a few times at CSULB and was becoming well known on the campus. But it was King —who was developing a reputation as a fine poet in her own right —Joan was most interested in contacting for a contribution to her maiden publication.

With her endearing, self-deprecating style and guileless nurturing spirit, Joan became a trusted friend and confidante to King and Bukowski, and often found herself in the unenviable position of acting as mediator during much of the duo's fiery dramas. This relationship became an entrée to friendships with other significant people in Bukowski's life, particularly his "women." This elite muse society would include poet and mother of his only child, Frances Dean Smith aka FrancEyE; poet, friend and lover, Ann Menebroker; and his second and last wife, Linda Beighle Bukowski. This left only two important women in Bukowski's life Joan hadn't met —Bukowski's first love, Jane Baker Cooney, and his first wife, Barbara Frye. I guarantee if they were still alive she would have their ear, as well.

I've joked with Joan about rounding up this eclectic group of femmes for a "Bukowski's WOMEN Tour." Can you imagine? Joan would most likely find herself again as referee, while dodging flying grimalkin fur. She is the nucleus that binds us—a testament to the respect and affection we hold for her and her superior diplomatic skills.

I had the privilege of meeting Joan in 1976. Although my recollection is hazy from massive quantities of alcohol consumed at this particular event, I do recall she was (and still is) a stunningly beautiful woman. But it wasn't her physical appearance that remained in my pickled memory bank—it was the warmth and consideration she showed toward a young, insecure red-haired girl in the company of her favorite poet, Charles Bukowski.

On July 11, 1976, Bukowski was scheduled to read at the legendary Troubadour nightclub in West Hollywood. As was the custom before each performance, Buk and I would arrive early in order to tip a few in the nearest bar before show time. He hated these appearances and would become sick with anxiety, often causing him to literally vomit while waiting in the wings. Witnessing his angst would also give me a sympathetic case of nerves. Our antidote was to douse the jitters with as many adult beverages we could down up to the moment they announced him on stage.

While medicating in the Troubadour's cocktail lounge, we were joined by a nondescript man and his lovely date, introduced to me as Joan Jobe Smith. I knew nothing about her—or her relationship to Bukowski, and didn't care to find out. As a rule, I was not comfortable with Buk's "friends"—either because I found them pretentious and dismissive, and/or because he always seemed to feel the need to create some unwarranted melodrama during, or shortly after, these gatherings.

But Joan was different. I liked her immediately. She had an aura of sweetness about her, and treated me with the same deference she showed Bukowski. Though our meeting was brief, and the conversation clouded by drink, she left me with a warm, positive impression.

Almost two decades would pass before I learned more about the kind woman who had sat beside me in the Troubadour lounge.

Shortly after Bukowski's death in 1994, I became aware of the auction Internet site known as *eBay*. I was fascinated to discover all the Buk memorabilia for sale on the site. One item in particular caught my eye—a special *Pearl* edition festschrift in honor of Charles Bukowski, published in 1995, and edited by *Joan Jobe Smith*, titled *Das Ist Alles*. I placed the winning bid, and when it arrived only then did I realize what an amazing talent she is. Aside from poems and art by Bukowski, the booklet also featured short stories and poetry written by Bukowski's notable friends and acquaintances, including Joan. I found her contributions as earthy, relatable, and enchanting as the delightful person I recalled meeting twenty years prior.

I tried locating more of her work. I placed orders for her out-of-print books on Amazon.com without success. Fortunately, I was able to find a copy of her *Bukowski Boulevard*, published in 1999, and later a couple copies of her *Bukowski Review* on the same auction site. I fell in love with her original lyrical writing style. Her words so vivacious and lively, like cool jazz bebopping on a page. She can turn the most serious subject into a lilting dance, ending with a dip and a smile.

I thought of Joan again in 2008 while writing my memoir, *Charles Bukowski's Scarlet*. When it came time to recall the events of Buk's Troubadour reading, many segments of that evening came to me in vivid detail. But no matter how hard I tried to transport myself back to the bar scene, specific details remained hazy. I could only recall the general impression she'd left on me—but not what she had looked like or what we'd discussed. I made an attempt to contact her through some of my Bukowski connections. I wanted to compare notes before writing this particular segment, but, again, she eluded me.

It wasn't until June 2010, when I received a call from my publisher Al Berlinski asking permission to give Joan my email address that we would finally connect again. She had read my book and wanted to meet for an interview. I arranged to have lunch with her and her husband, Fred Voss (also a great writer), at Canter's Restaurant in West Hollywood.

When I arrived, I was struck by how petite she is. After reading her work, my image of her was so dynamic I expected to meet a physically imposing Amazon. Instead, there sat a gorgeous *delicate flower* with the same sweet spirit and high-octane personality that dazzled me thirty-four years ago. The three of us exchanged our books for signing and had a few laughs recounting our Buk tales—while marveling at the irony of it all.

Joan also reminded me of our first encounter, which in this book will take place in Bukowski's living room. *Although I am certain Joan's memory is accurate, towards the end of my relationship with Hank I would often avoid situations where he had company for reasons previously mentioned. I'm certain there were others I've met under similar circumstances during this period I cannot now recall.*

Over the last two years, I have come to appreciate what an amazing woman Joan is, and the remarkable life she has lived. She managed to raise three children while working as a go-go girl during the turbulent 1960s and 70s, while simultaneously completing her college education. As a pioneering editor of the first literary magazine on the CSULB campus to initially encourage literary voices of women, Joan Jobe Smith remains an important figure in the history of the feminist movement and the poetry community, and continues to inspire and support a new generation of literary expression, male and female, through her works, and by selflessly showcasing others with the masterful assistance of her *Pearl* successor editor, Marilyn Johnson.

Although Joan has suffered much tragedy in her personal life, she continues to maintain a delightful sense of humor with an untarnished heart and spirit. Blessed with many gifts—including movie star looks—a lesser person would have taken a least-resistance path. She is a true survivor in every sense of the word.

Charles Bukowski emphasized the importance of style and grace in everything one does in life, and, as her mentor, the old man would not be disappointed. Like a sparkling bijou, Joan Jobe Smith is a gift to the world of art and humanity. It is a privilege to call her my friend.

"...as God said, crossing his legs, I see where I've made plenty of poets but not so much poetry."

CHARLES BUKOWSKI, "To the Whore Who Took My Poems"

AUTHOR'S NOTE
By Joan Jobe Smith

FOR MORE THAN A DECADE, 1973-1984, I ENJOYED—AND
endured—a passionate, profound, and platonic literary friendship
with the phenomenal poet-writer Charles Bukowski. As Passionate
Endurer, 1974-1976, I was a sounding board for He said/She said
descriptions of bombastic Bukowski's tumultuous love-hate affair
with his feisty paramour, poet-artist Linda King (the First Linda).
As ardent fan, get-up-and-go groupie, I enjoyed, 1972-1977, twelve
live performances by the profound Charles Bukowski at California
State University Long Beach, University of California Riverside,
Laguna Beach Moulton Theatre, the Golden Bear in Huntington
Beach, the Troubadour in West Hollywood, and Bodega Bar in
Long Beach, where I took copious notes for a future—I hoped—
M.A. thesis.

Privately, via letters and midnight telephone conversations,
Charles Bukowski became my gentle Mentor and my impish Muse. I
loved his art: his genius words, wisdom, and wit; I loved his easy
laughter. But most of all I loved how he loved us Women—his
nemeses and nymphs, his heroines and harridans, and I loved how he
wrote so much about us that his volumes of poems and prose depictions of Women and his undying love and lust for us equals Balzac,
Baudelaire, Tennessee Williams—and possibly Hugh Hefner—in
bountiful-inspired perpetuation of fabulous femme artifact. And I
was lucky enough to know some of Bukowski's fabled Women. And
now, Dear Reader, upon these pages I'd like to introduce them to
you—

TOO SEXY FOR CLOTHES
@ CAL STATE U LONG BEACH, 1973

Poem by Joan Jobe Smith

Everyone was crazy in 1973 streaking everywhere
taking their clothes off and going naked at love-ins,
sometimes across the stage at the Academy Awards
and every Friday at Cal State U Long Beach students
streaked across campus, one day the Science Majors:
Einstein, Isaac Newton, Pierre and Marie Curie, Louis
Pasteur, a slide rule dangling from his groin and the
next week the naked Art Majors: Monet, Picasso,
Michelangelo, Georgia O'Keefe, van Gogh with big
amber sunflowers painted all over his pink naked bod
while the rest of the students who wore clothes sat
on the grass watching, applauding and smoking pot
and some of the professors were too sexy for their
clothes, too, dated their young students, an A for a lay.
What was this world coming to? I'd never seen anything
like it and I'd been a go-go girl for 7 years, had come
back to college for knowledge, literally clean up my act,
learn sense and sensibility and To be or not to be. Not be
too sexy for my clothes, learn to streak naked. I hated
how the times were a'changin' and then it all got worse
that awful day that 19-year-old wannabe-Rimbaud in
my poetry writing class organized for next Friday a
Poet Streaking Party: all us poets to meet at the rest
rooms in the student union to take off all our clothes.
Then, all us Emily Dickinsons, Sylvia Plaths, Rod Mc
Kuens, T.S. Eliots, Walt Whitmans and e e cummings
amongst us were to run naked together down the stairs
to the bookstore, then run naked past the grassy area,
then to the English Department to run naked up and
down the stairs. "It'll be a blast! Out of sight!" said
Rimbaud. But none of us poets showed up. So come
Monday our Poetry Prof Dr. Lee thanked us all for not

streaking, praised us for being dignified English Majors and then chuckled impishly as he held up a new book by a new writer Charles Bukowski: *Erections, Ejaculations, Exhibitions and General Tales of Ordinary Madness.*
For sale at CSULB's bookstore. Roll over, Jane Austen.
Bob Dylan, too, because times were a'changin' again.

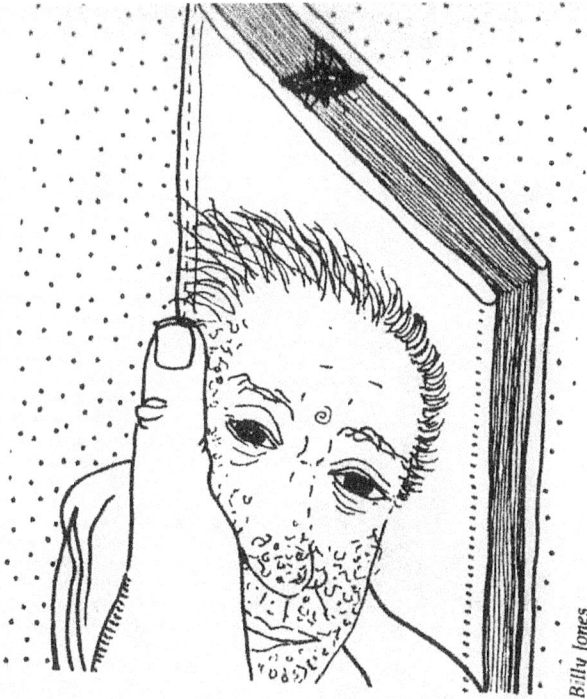

"Aren't you going to kiss me goodbye?"
CHARLES BUKOWSKI

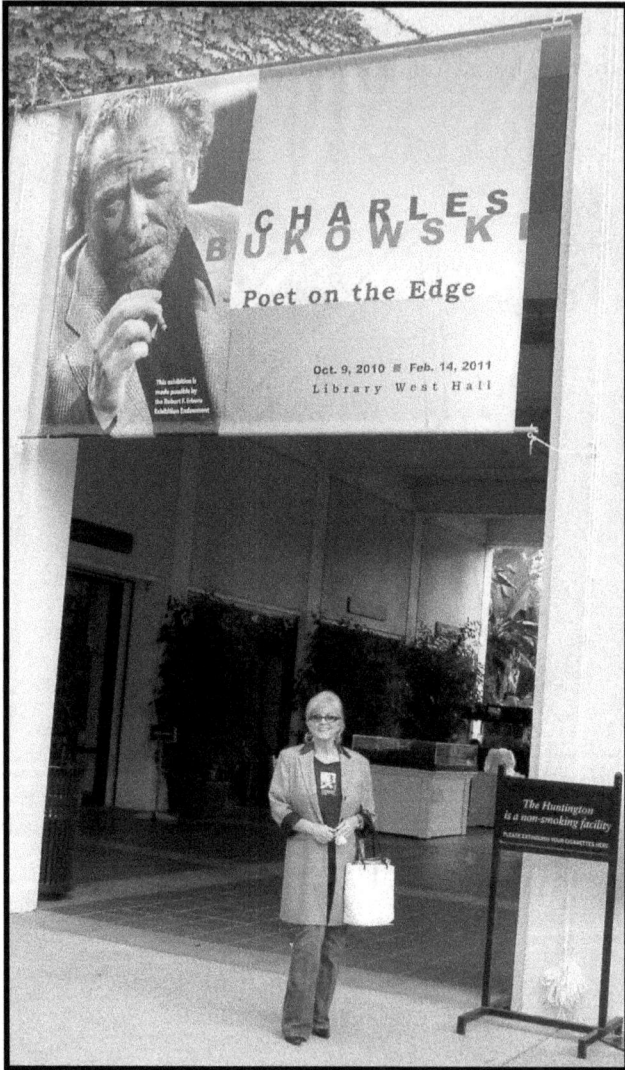

Pamela "Cupcakes" Miller Wood at the Huntington Library, October 2010.

LOVE AMONGST CHARLES BUKOWSKI & THE THREE SCARLETS:
Pamela "Cupcakes" Miller Wood Interview
By Joan Jobe Smith (June 19, 2010)

CHARLES BUKOWSKI WAS THE FIRST AUTHOR THAT I EVER wanted to meet, and got to do so, after reading in 1972 his book of poetry, *The Days Run Away Like Wild Horses Over the Hills*. Not many things more fun for a literature lover or college student with an English major like I was in 1972 than meeting a writer whose work has captured his/her heart in its hand. You want to ask: "How did you do it? Why do you do it?" You need to know these things—if you're a certain kind of lit lover. And I am.

In 2010, after reading *Charles Bukowski's Scarlet: A Memoir* by Pamela "Cupcakes" Wood—the latest Bukowski homage/ exposé from Allen Berlinski's Sun Dog Press—penned by the mythical "Scarlet" herself, Bukowski's Beautiful-Girl-Who-Got-Away and the most attractive of Berlinski's prodigious list of writers ranging from True Grit Dan Fante to Bukowski been-there biographers, I got that need to Meet the Author again. Though I'd been publishing *Pearl* since 1974, published four issues of *Bukowski Review* (2000-2005), and had met countless authors by then—even some poet laureates, OBEs, and Pulitzer Prizers—and even though I'd met Pamela "Cupcakes" Wood in July 1976, I just had to meet her again. Ask her, "Why did you write this?" *She* had been Bukowski's muse that Year of the Dragon that had been the United States of America's Bicentennial, 1976. In 2010, she'd turned the tables, turned Bukowski into *her* Muse.

Finally sticking up for herself after all those years, her Redhead Redemption, the first of Bukowski's Women to publish a prose memoir, the one about whom Bukowski had written, "Who brought me the knife of laughter," Pamela "Cupcakes" Wood delivered ably and winsomely some fast/fun reading. As Bukowski's real-life girl next door when she fortuitously lived on Carlton Way in 1975-76, in this memoir, Cupcakes has given readers and Bukowski fans a fresh crop of fertile Bukowski-and-Me conversation, fabulous, never-before-seen photographs, and reliable shit-faced shenanigans surreal performed perfectly on the page and on cue by the ever-pixilated, love-and-booze-besotted Charles Bukowski ranting profane and coarse, of course—the Eternal Antagonist. Fascinating as always—but, this time, more so. And Cupcakes captured him with her elegant heart and portrayed him properly—and lovingly, gracefully—with her gentle pen.

Then I came to Chapter 29 where the Almost-Young Me makes a cameo appearance at the Troubadour nightclub in Hollywood, July 11, 1976. Not quite the way I'd remembered it, though. Memory, however, is always in the eye of the hurricane typewriter. Truth in the mouth of the loudest speaker. No one should dare critique another's reconstruction of Remembrances Past, especially that raunchy, complicated often sinister decade of the get-it-on, do-it-in-the-road, love-the-one-you're-with Swinging 1970s.

Cupcakes and I had actually met the night before at Bukowski's cluttered apartment. I was with my *Pearl* co-editor Marilyn Johnson and a very rich man who wanted to start up a new press and talked me into introducing him to Bukowski so he could offer him a publishing deal better than what Bukowski had with John Martin's Black Sparrow Press. July 10, 1976, Cupcakes and her girlfriend Georgia, all dolled up and on their way to a swinging party, stopped by to say goodbye to Bukowski who groaned, much preferring their company to ours. But back to the Troubadour, July 11, 1976.

Cupcakes was drinking a lot of champagne—and so was I—paid for by Very Rich Man, while she, Bukowski, VRM, and I shared a café table in the crowded Troubadour bar. VRM, who'd brought a wad of papers, a contract for Buk to sign, pitched again his publishing deal to Bukowski who was opening that night at the Troubadour for an up-and-coming new comedian, Steve Martin. Cupcakes giggled and smiled as bright and pretty as a Rabbit Moon. Restless, squirming with boredom in her seat, while VRM blabbed on. When I turned to talk to her, she'd mysteriously disappeared in the Troubadour's maddening crowd. She was a thin little thing, wore tight hippie chick, puddling bellbottomed jeans and a low-cut tank top that revealed a lovely, pink bosom when it plumped from the strawberry shawl of her long, beautiful hair. One week after America celebrated its big, boastful Bicentennial, Elton John crocodile rocked, Frank Sinatra did it His Way, and Charles Bukowski still had one foot in Bohemia, but the other pointed at impending literary fame and prosperity that would lead him to Yuppieville and Nouveau Riche Beyond.

When VRM went to the men's room, leaving Bukowski and me alone, Buk grumbled, yet whined: "Cupcakes's strung out." He tattled on Cupcakes like a little boy on a playground reporting a bully. "Taking uppers, you name it," he gossiped on, finking on his sweetie—what a cad, the stewed stewpot calling the demitasse black. I thought Cupcakes was just tipsy on champagne, like I was. The ungallant Bukowski lied a lot about his Women, most of it self-aggrandizing hyperbole, as I already knew from the three years I'd known him and Linda King together. Linda had left him six months ago, for good. Just a week before, Cupcakes moved in next door to Bukowski on Carlton Way.

Whatever was going on drug-wise or champagne-wise that night with the laughing, wide-eyed, dimpled and vivacious Cupcakes with all the flowing, flaming hair, too sexy for her clothes of tight jeans and tank top, Cupcakes resembled every young, cool, hip, and insouciant L.A. Woman, summer of 1976 hot to trot and do her own thing.

Busy at the time polishing up his next Black Sparrow kiss-and-tell book *Women,* telling it all His Way—as always, as the hellzapopping Hank Chinaski—Bukowski will write me in a month: "Wrote about you, too, kid, but you're not a very interesting woman, so I dumped you." I've always been grateful he dumped me, made me an outtake. I was merely one of his many devotee, peripheral editor-publishers, and an occasional telephone flirtation when lonely times he drank too much and called long distance from his dump in Hollywood to my house in suburbia. And many of the women in his book *Women* were not so kindly or accurately presented. (I know because I knew most of them.) The character "Tammie" resembled the real Pamela "Cupcakes" Wood not the least little bit.

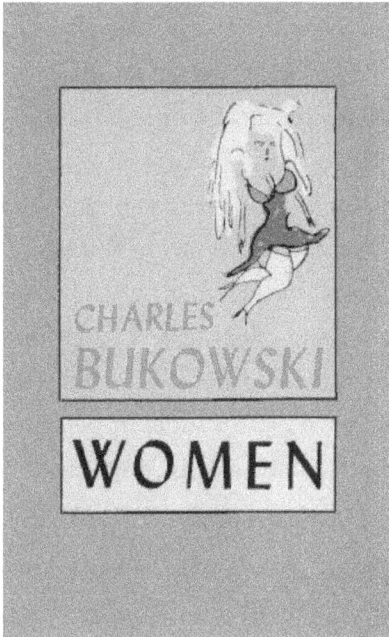

Black Sparrow Press published Charles Bukowski's novel *Women* in 1978.

July 11, 1976, Bukowski'd been unusually cordial and kind to me, not belligerent and lecherous as he often was. This night, he was sober and in a good mood—because he was In Love with Cupcakes, truly in love with this sweet, sexy little redheaded thing thirty-two years his junior. Also, I suspected, his solicitous cordiality to me was a phony persona so's to make the young Cupcakes jealous. He kept leaning toward me, *tête-à-tête,* as if asking me sotto voce deep personal secrets, possibly sexy ones, when he was really asking me about my small press magazine, *Pearl,* my plans for the future. I'd closed shop in 1975 after the third issue in which Bukowski and his then-girlfriend Linda King were featured, their love poems plus a sexy picture of them lying in a waterbed, kissing. *Pearl4* would have featured Anaïs Nin's unpublished stories and some of her poems. Anaïs and I had become brief telephone friends, having met via feminist poet Rochelle Holt. But Anaïs Nin became ill with cancer, too weak to send me her work, so I decided to publish an all-men poet "Male Chauvinist Pig"-themed issue, with Bukowski's drawing on the cover titled "Men's Lib Poster" that he drew especially for *Pearl:* a portrait of me as a giantess next to a six-inch man, a cartoon Bukowski. But I ran out of money to publish it, and when I mentioned my impecunity to Bukowski, he suddenly bellowed: *"Where's my Cupcakes!?"* He'd just noticed she'd split the scene, no doubt bored by his nice-guy nearness to me.

So crowded and noisy in the Troubadour preshow bar (actress Carrie Snodgrass sat nearby), no one flinched or wondered if some drunk thought he was in a bakery. Buk had conserved his energies all day by limiting his alcohol consumption; he wanted to give a good, sober, and sane performance that night—they were paying him a thrilling thousand dollars, nearly a year's worth of rent on his cluttered pad on Carlton Way—but he suddenly looked and acted drugged-out and crazed. Bukowski stood up and looked all around. "Cupcakes's gone! She's run out on me again! That little—" But suddenly Cupcakes appeared. And so did VRM. Both of them smiling.

"Smarmy asshole," Bukowski grumbled about VRM. "Where'd you meet this prick?"

As Bukowski and Cupcakes departed to go to the Green Room, unwind and prep preshow, VRM gave the cocktail waitress a hundred-dollar bill to bring us two more bottles of champagne, keep the change, then shoved his big fat wallet—crammed with the two thousand dollars worth of hundreds he kept on a chain—back into his front pocket, making him look as testicular, and undoubtedly deliberately, encumbered as a horse.

Hard to get, Buk had declined VRM's offer the previous night, even after he promised to make Buk rich—hardbound covers on all his books, not just the special editions, to class him up, plus appearances on the Johnny Carson Show and lounge readings in Las Vegas. He'd make Bukowski more famous than Rod McKuen and John Lennon put together. "I hate this son of a bitch," Bukowski whispered to me the night before. He hated all men richer, better looking, or taller than he was. But Bukowski kept his cool; VRM had just enriched his life with bribes—cases of Chianti and beer. He might've hated the gift-giver, but he loved the schmooze and booze.

Last night, in his cluttered Carlton Way apartment, Bukowski wouldn't even take five hundred dollars VRM offered him for a copy of *Scarlet*—his just-out Black Sparrow signed limited edition, just one hundred available, book of love-and-lust poems about Pamela "Cupcakes" Wood, priced at one hundred dollars. A beautiful, slim, hardbound ode to his beautiful, scarlet-haired Cupcakes. Marilyn, VRM, and I watched Bukowski lovingly, elegantly autograph a stack of them while we drank Chianti with him. "Wow! How beautiful!" I exclaimed. "Reminiscent of D.H. Lawrence's special editions," I said, awed by the book. "William Blake did this too."

"Mine's *better* than theirs!" Bukowski said—never at a loss for Confidence.

When I tried to thumb through one, read a poem, one of his loving-Scarlet poems, Bukowski snatched it away, growled at me: "You'll get it dirty!"

Next time I'd see another *Scarlet* would be in 1999, twenty-three years later; it'd be locked up, under glass at Red Skodolsky's Hollywood bookstore, price: one thousand dollars.

Back at the Troubadour, circa 1976, Bukowski got VRM, Cupcakes, and me front-row seats, a table, four chairs next to the stage. VRM waved big-spenderly again—his five-karat diamond pinky ring sparkling à la Lucy in the Sky—for two more bottles of pricy champagne, plus bottles of Michelob beer for Bukowski to reach for from the stage when he wanted one. When the stage lights went down and the spotlight shined bright, from the side of the stage, Cupcakes appeared, prancing, laughing, pink-skinned, hair seeming on fire, and said into the microphone, "Bukowski's performance has been cancelled!"

Most of the audience went silent, some groaned. Then Cupcakes giggled and said, "Only kidding! Ladies and gentlemen, here he is—*Charles Bukowski!*" And Bukowski lumbered onto the stage to riotous applause.

At the microphone, he said: "Harrr. That's my new gimmick! They just keep gettin' younger and younger!" Everyone roared with laughter as Cupcakes stepped off the stage, quietly nudged through the chairs, away from the super-bright stage lights, and headed for the long bar, way back, in the dark-dark side of the cavernous room. Then Charles Bukowski laughed into the microphone, as he usually did just before he began to read his poetry, and thus began his premiere performance at the Troubadour—and the place was packed, standing room only. Everyone applauded loudly at the end of each of his good poems. Laughed at his irony, his wit, raunch, and life absurdities. This Swinging Seventies drinking/stoned-and-in-sin crowd loved him, loved being entertained.

When Bukowski began to read his Cupcakes Poems, she shouted out from the black back area near the back exit: *"That's about me!"* And everyone laughed.

Then Bukowski replied, lovingly, almost-paternally in his deep, rich, nasally-god voice, a cross between W.C. Fields and Zeus: "Yes, dear, that was about you." He smiled, showing big white teeth. And then he read on. This call-and-response always entertained. I'd seen this sugar-schtick, this pleasant improv several times at Bukowski's readings, 1972-1975, when his True Love and Main Muse had been Linda King. But this was novice Cupcakes's premiere performance, too, at the Troubadour; she was young, a shaky newbie at this, and wasn't quite the willing and wanton enthusiast Linda King had been. VRM got up—again—to use the men's room. But this time VRM didn't come back.

When Bukowski read another new Scarlet poem, Cupcakes didn't shout out or answer when he called out her name.

Shielding his eyes to squint through the thick spotlight to find her out there in the dark someplace, he bellowed into the crowd: *"Where are you, Cupcakes?!"*

No answer. No Scarlet. No Cupcakes. They'd both left the building, run out on him again, but Bukowski didn't know that— yet. He laughed har-har and read more. His jutting Neanderthal brow made his shaded eyes look like two big black spoon-shaped moons. (In 1999, I will buy for my poet husband Fred Voss a T-shirt with "Love Is a Dog from Hell" written on it, and Bukowski's portrait looking the way Buk did July 11, 1976.) Half an hour later, when the poetry was over and the lights turned back on, VRM and Cupcakes were still missing in action. Both of them had missed two-thirds of the show. Next to the empty stage, Bukowski stood shoulder-to-shoulder with me while he autographed books, Buk forlorn, missing Cupcakes. (Near this very spot in September, after an encore performance at the Troubadour, he would meet his future wife, Linda Lee Beighle when she asks for his autograph and gives him her telephone number.)

July 11, 1976, near midnight, Bukowski looked older but no wiser than his almost-fifty-six years. Resembling an ancient satyr I'd once seen in a Reubens painting at the Getty Museum, hirsute, muscular Bukowski slumped while he stood there and held limply an empty beer bottle, as useless to him now as an ancient, out-of-tune satyr's flute. The Show was over; floodlights now blasted the smoke-filled Troubadour, and his Muse, his mythical scarlet wood nymph nowhere in sight amongst the mute trumpets of the bright. I had no way home—I had been stranded by VRM.

When I mentioned this to Bukowski, he grumbled he'd take me home with him, which meant I'd have to spend the night with him—a possibility neither of us looked forward to. I knew how Bukowski loved to be with the one he loved, not with the one he was with. "I LOVE WOMEN," he'd once written me. "Mostly when they love ME." I loved Bukowski, all right, his poetry, that is, but—suddenly, luckily, VRM showed up, coming in the Troubadour back door exit from the alley out back. Claimed he'd seen Scarlet stagger out to the alley, looking sick, so he followed her to lend a helping hand but couldn't find her. She'd disappeared into thin air. Locked out, the management wouldn't let him in the front door because the place was sold out, standing room only. VRM acted angry and disappointed.

Memory and Truth being what they are: fragile and faraway until seemingly becoming fabrications, deep-hearted and surreal, I had to see Cupcakes again, in person, see if she was really real then and now, compare notes of our knock-about knowledge of that self-styled Love Dog from Hell, Henry Charles Bukowski.

And here comes Cupcakes now: June 19, 2010, dressed in L.A. Woman go-getter careerist chic—sexy high-high heels, slinky slacks, epauletted leather jacket—she totes an airtight plastic u-haul bucket containing not the priceless treasure of Spanish gold doubloons but the comparable bounty of her private paper collection of signed Bukowski books. Still a petite, shapely, beautiful girl, Cupcakes plops down the plastic, the thud of it echoing out of our booth at Canters, L.A.'s famous delicatessen that's served kosher 24-7 ever since Eddie Cantor and the Beatles. Cupcakes' once-scarlet hair glows creamy blonde now, and her golden hoop earrings sparkle first-day-of-California-Girl-summer, which this June 19, 2010 day almost is.

Pamela "Cupcakes" Miller Wood (right) signs a copy of her memoir, *Charles Bukowski's Scarlet,* for Joan Jobe Smith.

While she gently unwraps her precious cargo: a copy of *Scarlet* she was offered five thousand dollars for ten years ago, she smiles at me. Then she lets me hold this precious book in my hands third time in my life I've laid eyes on a copy.

"Wow," I say again, thirty-four years later, in 2010, with the same amazed admiration I had in 1976—just before Charles Bukowski, the author, snatched it away, Antagonist Eternal. This time I sit in the Bukowski triangle of three Scarlets: Scarlet, the Muse; *Scarlet*, the Memoir; and *Scarlet*, the Ode to Love, which begins with Charles Bukowski's tender dedication:

> *"For the girl who made me feel that feeling*
>
> *which comes so seldom in a lifetime—"*

Cupcakes, aka Pamela Miller Wood, girl déjà vu, smiles, her dimples still there—just as I'd remembered them all these years. And then I begin to conduct my interview with this fascinating, beautiful creature, and we begin to speak of Love Amongst Charles Bukowski and the Three Fabulous Scarlets...

CUPCAKES INTERVIEW

JOAN JOBE SMITH: Cupcakes, uh, I mean Pam, your just-out memoir from Sun Dog Press, *Scarlet,* in which world-famous poet Charles Bukowski played a significant role for nearly two years of your young life, is the most fascinating biography I've read in a long time. You've captured a big chunk of Swinging Seventies gritty reality and showed ably and winsomely what it was like back then to be a single mom of twenty-four with a baby to care for in the raunchy midst of all the crazy, let-it-all-hang-out, love-the-one-you're-with happenings in that L.A.-Hollywood backdrop. What inspired you to tell your true story now, after all these years that have run away like wild horses over the hills?

PAMELA MILLER WOOD: Hi Joan. First, thank you for your kind words about my memoir. I consider this high praise coming from someone who personally knew Bukowski and whose work I admire. And please feel free to call me Cupcakes; since my book release, all my friends do.

The idea of writing my memoir did not occur to me until 1997 after being approached by two gentlemen on separate occasions, both requesting an interview for their respective Bukowski projects; John Dullaghan, who produced the documentary, "Born into This," and Howard Sounes, author of the Bukowski biography, *Locked in the Arms of a Crazy Life.* At that time, aside from reading *Women* and viewing *Barfly,* I had not followed his career since we parted ways in 1977. I was surprised they felt I played a significant enough role in his life to seek me out. Both pointed to several poems, letters, and other material written after our split, which I found stunning.

Though, I admit not being thrilled about his painting a less-than-flattering portrait of my character in *Women,* I figured this was his way of getting back at me for a freshly wounded ego. "Tammie" was such a preposterous flibbertigibbet—and the entire book so hilarious—I found it hard to be angry with him. I imagined him typing those scenes and thinking, *oh yeah, that's a good one...this will really get her pink panties in a twist, ha, ha, ha...*

However, after reading several pieces, the letters in particular—so full of venom and disdain, I was upset. I felt more confused than angry—mostly over the common thread of deception and wickedness he attributes to my true character while we were together. The more vile the insult, the sadder I felt. Not for me—for him. It broke my heart to think he felt the need to demonize me in such an ugly fashion. Not that I expected to read glowing tributes, but it was so far removed from my recollection that I even found myself wondering if I had possibly blocked out portions of our affair as some sort of defense mechanism.

An angel, I was not, but neither was I the grubby, conniving nymph he so frequently suggests. Believe me, I have many flaws, but vicious and manipulative are not part of my makeup; both involve too much work. I supposed by convincing himself that I was a dirty rat, maybe he was better off without me, right? No offense to Buk, but if I *were* that type of woman, I would have focused my vamping powers on someone who actually had money and a much more comfortable, appetizing environment in which to languish. I could not understand why he felt this way, real, or fabricated.

It was my need to find some answers about that period in my life that prompted this memoir. I decided to write it primarily for me—like a diary. I knew I had to be painfully honest and objective if I was to learn anything about our relationship and myself.

It would take ten years, inspired by the worst tragedy of my adult life, to find the time to write this book. I've been working in the real estate business since 1977. In 1997, the Los Angeles market was catching fire. I was working twelve, sometimes fourteen hours a day, seven days a week. It was pure insanity. It wasn't until 2005, when my sister died of a brain tumor, that I realized how fragile and unpredictable life is. She was forty-seven years old when diagnosed in 2002, one month after my brother died of a drug overdose. He was fifty-four. Though my brother's death was sad, given his life-style, it was not unexpected. My sister Tracey was a joyful, healthy, vibrant, successful woman, with two beautiful young daughters. She had the world at her feet—then BOOM!—her life shattered in an instant. Not only confronted with my own mortality, I was consumed with inconsolable grief. I began to reevaluate everything. I made a bucket list, and decided once I had enough money set aside to get through a year without working I would quit my job and do whatever I damn well pleased. That day came in November 2007. I figured this would be the best time to write the book while all my faculties were still in working order.

JJS: Your young life would make a fabulous movie. What actors today would you pick as suitable to play Bukowski? Yourself?

PMW: Without a doubt, Jack Nicholson would be my first choice. Hollywood can make anyone look the part with makeup, but to capture the essence of someone who actually existed is difficult. Nicholson embodies many of the same personality traits as Bukowski, including his impish devil-dog quality. Nicholson also has the wide-ranging talent necessary to carry off the role of such a complex character. Runners-up would be Sean Penn, Robert Downey, Jr., and Bill Murray.

I don't consider my young self in the same league as these beautiful women, but, once again, they possess some of the Cupcakes *essence*. They are: Christina Hendricks, Kate Hudson, and maybe Kristen Stewart. Lindsay Lohan would have made my list a couple years ago, but, sadly, appears to be going through now what I was then.

JJS: What actors of 1976, if you'd published your *Scarlet* back then?

PMW: Hmm, that's a tough one. Nicholson may have been too young then. Maybe William Holden, Gene Hackman, or Orson Welles; Valerie Perrine, Susan Sarandon, or Ann-Margret.

JJS: What's the most important thing about you as young Pamela/Cupcakes you'd like the readers to know?

PMW: As I mentioned in the first answer, I wasn't a schemer. That takes more brains, effort, and patience than I had then, or now, and I would not find plotting to take advantage of anyone the least bit satisfying. That's probably why I'm such a lousy chess player. Don't get me wrong; I could be a brat, but always a well-intentioned one who never set out to deliberately hurt another.

JJS: How about Pamela Wood, go-getter career woman, of now?

PMW: The most important thing about me now that I'd like the readers to know?—honestly?—nothing. I know that may sound rude, but I don't intend it to. I've always been pathologically private about my personal life. I'm sure that sounds ridiculous having just written a book full of extremely intimate details, but that was a life-time ago—

JJS: If Bukowski were still alive and wrote an Apologia to the women he skewered in his 1977 *Women,* what anecdote about you would you like to see revised?

PMW: Interesting question…Given all the immoral sexual behavior, and the lack of any sense of decency, intelligence or conscience he assigns to the character Tammie, you may find this hard to believe, but I was most offended by the anti-Semitic remark she makes in the New York segment. That, to me, was obscene. The rest was so hilarious that I had to laugh.

JJS: What kind of flowers and what color would you want him to bring to you when he begged your forgiveness for his being such a Ham on Rye in 1976?

PMW: A bouquet of pimpernels—scarlet, of course. Seriously, pink Gerbera daisies—I love them! There is something so sweet and whimsical about them. They always make me smile. Then, again, any flowers sent my way make me smile.

JJS: When a little girl, I loved dolls, believed in dolls, collected them. If I were to find a Bukowski's Women Doll Series, what would your Cupcakes Doll look like? Barbie lookalike, G.I. Jane, Raggedy Ann, Cabbage Patch, Dora the Explorer?

PMW: All the above in the form of a life-sized blowup doll.

JJS: What is your favorite Bukowski poem/book?

PMW: My favorite poem is "Shoelace." I relate to that poem daily. My favorite novel is a tossup between *Hollywood* and *Women*—followed by *Ham On Rye, Post Office, Factotum,* and *Pulp.* I also get a huge kick out of his illustrated works—*The Day it Snowed in LA, Bring Me Your Love,* and *Dear Mr. Bukowski* still crack me up—no matter how many times I read them.

JJS: You're in L.A. real estate sales now. You know L.A. maybe more than anyone. What s the best part of the part you like best?

PMW: Besides the awesome wonder of the Pacific Ocean, I would have to say the West Side. In my opinion, this is the hub of LA culture. Museums, art galleries, fine restaurants, latest fashions—they're all there. You also have very trendy pockets, like Melrose Avenue, full of LA-centric shops. Even the best hospital, Cedars Sinai, is located there. The atmosphere is full of creative energy. Many people I meet there remind me more of New Yorkers; sophisticated, yet down to earth. Sometimes I'll hop in my car and drive twenty miles to the west side with no particular destination in mind just because I find it exhilarating.

JJS: How did knowing Charles Bukowski interfere with or enhance your life?

PMW: Very good question. Except for my daughter wondering what her mommy was doing with that strange-looking old man who lived in that icky apartment, and my last husband almost calling off our wedding after reading *Women,* can't say he interfered with my life. After all, I chose to be with him. He did enhance my life in many ways.

Aside from the obvious benefits of living with a literary genius—you may find this surprising—I believe his decision to stop bailing me out of difficult situations facilitated my road to recovery. That may not have been the true motivation behind his tough love, but it was the best thing he could have done for me. Naturally, I didn't see it that way at the time, but now realize what an amazing gift that was.

JJS: What flavors of cupcakes are you?

PMW: Then…Naughty & Nutty Red Velvet, Carpet Matches the Drapes Grape, Hoochie Mama Mint, Buk's Blueberry Banana—Now… Get Off My Lawn Lemon or Beta Blocking Butter Cream with a dollop of Lipitor or Butterscotch Botox with Retinol Cream Icing …ha!

JJS: Pamela, uh, I mean Cupcakes, this has been so much fun, meeting you again, dishing and dissing Bukowski, sitting here at Canter's nearly thirty-four years after we last saw each other at the Troubadour, July 11, 1976, you with your own book called *Scarlet*—your exhilarating, entertaining memoir about your incredible life with and without Charles Bukowski—autographing copies the way I watched Bukowski autograph the first *Scarlet* he wrote about you in 1976. Thank you, Cupcakes, for being so forthcoming with your answers. I could ask you questions all day. But I see our server snubbing us, not refilling your coffee cup. Before we go, though, I think I hear Bukowski right now har-harring amongst the trumpets, saying to you about your fabulous book *Scarlet:* "Way to go, baby." If he really were here right now noshing a ham on rye and chugging a German beer, what do you think Bukowski would say to you?

PMW: "Not bad, Red, not bad at all. See, I taught you well. This old man's proud of ya, kid!"

Pamela "Cupcakes" Wood, Fred Voss, and Joan Jobe Smith at The Frolic Room, Los Angeles, November 1, 2010.

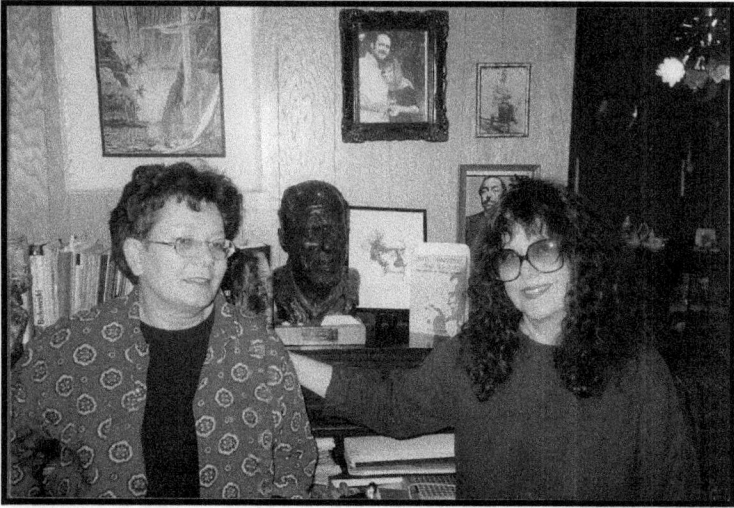

Linda King (left) and Joan Jobe Smith, circa 2000, with a copy of Bukowski's head that King sculpted in 1972. In background: Bukowski portrait by David Hernandez and copy of *Art, Survival and So Forth: The poetry of Charles* Bukowski by Jules Smith (Wrecking Ball Press, UK).

CHARLES BUKOWSKI:

The Poet as Entertainer

By Joan Jobe Smith

Unbelievable to think that here I am, in 2012, half of my lifetime plus two years later, rewriting this piece I first drafted in August 1975, when I was a law student. Seventeen long years later, after I dropped out of law school, received a Master of Fine Arts in fiction writing from the University of California Irvine and married the poet Fred Voss. A portion appeared in *Sure—The Charles Bukowski Newsletter* #4, 1992. In the spring 1994 issue of *Chiron Review*, "The Poet As Entertainer" was published *in toto* as a column I wrote called "Swimming in the Word Stew."

In autumn 1974, when a near-graduate of California State University Long Beach, I proposed the idea of "The Poet As Entertainer" as a thesis subject for a master's degree—with Charles Bukowski's hearty approval and his magnanimous offer of collaborative cooperation. But the powers in charge at CSULB rejected my idea as not only lacking sufficient literary merit to justify a thesis about such a controversial writer of undocumented academic value but also derided the concept of *The Poet As Entertainer* as inconsequential. Now here's this ancient piece I wrote long ago—my mere rosebud notion that never bloomed, that a poet could be entertaining, precluding the 1990s emergence of the performance poets and slam poets—originally inspired by Charles Bukowski, one of the first entertainer poets, along with Dylan Thomas. This might've evolved into a landmark and possibly remarkable thesis, and exists now as merely a small piece of Bukowski historical data for his many fans who never had the good fortune to see and hear in person the amazing man read some of the most extraordinary and entertaining poetry ever written or performed.

WOMEN WERE ESPECIALLY UNKIND TO CHARLES BUKOWSKI that bright, blue, beautiful afternoon of August 15, 1975, the day before Bukowski's fifty-fifth birthday. Sunshine-made diamonds danced at four o'clock p.m. on the aquamarine Pacific Ocean down the road from the Moulton Theatre in Laguna Beach, California, while Bukowski sat frowning in the far-corner seats of the dark last row, watching the audience meander into the small theater.

"Feminists! Look at them—" Bukowski whispered to his girl-friend Linda King and me as he sat between us. "Women's libbers. They're gonna kill me, I know it."

Already inebriated, drinking beer since breakfast, Bukowski grabbed another pop-top can of his favorite red-and-white-labeled cheap beer from his six-pack and flagrantly snapped it open—*pop! spit!* spat the beer almost loud as gunfire as it echoed off the walls of the Moulton Theatre and stunk up a wide circle with its skunk-reeking stench.

Some of the spew splattered nastily onto the pricy pale blue denim pseudo-hippie-chick tatterdemalion jacket and bellbottom jeans of one woman, the one with permed frizzy hair—a Billie Jean King lookalike. She jerked her neck and gave Bukowski a dirty look as he chugged a long drink of beer; quickly, Billie Jean King stepped away to catch up with her female companions, many intellectual-looking types wearing granny glasses, long skirts with beach-set, mode-o-day, Birkinstock sandals.

A nattily dressed man who walked behind them—wearing an ascot and a white tennis sweater shawl over the shoulders of his pink Brooks Brothers shirt that was tucked neatly into white linen trousers—stopped, eyed-up Bukowski's casual apparel of navy blue plaid shirt and dark tan corduroy pants, then glared at the noisy red and white beer can that seemed to glow in the dark. The carefully clad middle-aged gentleman shook his balding head as if he couldn't believe his eyes.

For sure, none of these fine, conservative, well-to-do folks of Laguna Beach and surrounding Orange County areas who'd voted for Richard Nixon in the last presidential election had ever seen the likes of Charles Bukowski. I was surprised when I heard that the Laguna Beach Arts Council had invited him to appear at their 3rd Annual Poetry Week that coincided with the popular, crowd-pleasing, and jam-packed Laguna Beach Festival of Arts. Last year, a dignified famous poet-&-Ph.D.-professor from a prestigious university back East had appeared. If that sartorial man had known that this drunken man chug-a-lugging a can of beer, this disheveled factotum who looked like an off-duty janitor or postal clerk, was the star of the show, he might've asked for a refund. Or possibly called a policeman.

At that moment, this was as good as it was going to get; that is, as good as Bukowski was going to be—etiquette-wise. For the past five years that he'd been doing poetry readings in bars, little theatres, colleges, and universities, he'd been accruing quite a poetry résumé, thanks to his notorious reputation for unpredictable, if not unsuitable behavior. Irrepressible, usually drunk at his readings, he had more surprises inside him than a psychotic Pandora's box. Sometimes, during a standing ovation of lit majors and profs, he'd inexplicably left the stage and didn't come back. Once, he vomited into a baby grand piano valued at ten thousand dollars.

In spite of such maniacal mythology, here he was in the mainstream. Undoubtedly, the 1972 Taylor Hackford documentary shown frequently on PBS and the fact that Bukowski's books of poetry and fiction starring superego-id Hank Chinaski were becoming well-read among the literati as well as readers-at-large were the main fascinating facts that prompted the genteel intelligentsia Laguna Beach art connoisseurs to stick their necks out and invite the most controversial American poet of 1975—or any year then or since—to read his poetry on their small, intimate, nearly parlor-sized stage, where a red-velvet-covered Baroque throne chair awaited the arrival of featured poet Charles Bukowski.

The women in the bright front row, the feminists, the women's libbers, buzzed competently, loudly, like a busy swarm of queen bees. Together, a rehearsed chorus, the ten or so of them pointed accusingly at us sitting in the dark back row.

"See? What'd I tell ya?" Bukowski groaned. "They wanna tear me a apart. That one with the frizzy hair. She's the ringleader. She's gonna give me shit. I'm sure of it."

They looked remarkably like the feminists I'd seen, autumn 1973, at Bukowski's CSULB reading—an entire front row that walked out in the middle of him reading a lascivious segment from his novel-in-progress, *Factotum*.

Almost his birthday, nervous and drunk to boot, he hadn't wanted to accept this gig in Laguna Beach.

"Goddamned red-necked country. They voted for Barry Goldwater and then that son of a bitch Richard Nixon, who lives just down the road in San Clemente," he grumbled to Linda King and me. "They're not gonna dig me. And it's a helluva long way from L.A. You're gonna have to drive me home, Linda. Maybe right now, baby. I'm drunk. I've had too many goddamn beers. I'm out of it. Look at those libbers. They keep looking at me. I feel like I'm gonna puke."

Instead, he snapped open another pop-top, the noise making others turn around to look at the dark last row. Bukowski toasted them with his foaming beer can. One of the front row women's libbers turned all the way around and shook her head at him, disgusted by the sight of him. "That one—" Bukowski spearheaded his beer can at her; she wore a Jane Fonda Hanoi Jane shag hairdo. "She wants to cut my balls off. She's probably got a switchblade in her purse. These women's libbers are mean babes, tough cookies."

Usually the middle-class suburban males gave Bukowski the most rowdy feedback. Backlash. Heckling, actually. Or the inebriated, young university frat boys. Most of his readings back then took place in bars. Bukowski's favorite habitat—next to his typewriter or bedroom. In May 1975, I'd seen him torn into, verbally abused by a pack of drunken Marines in Huntington Beach, at a nightclub across the Pacific Coast Highway from the Pier, the famous Golden' Bear where ten years before, in May 1966, Lenny Bruce had given one of his last performances, busted for obscenity right on the stage, dragged off to jail in handcuffs. The next night, I went to see Lenny Bruce only to find him replaced by the sweet, sedate—and blind—Jose Feliciano with his gentle guide dog resting at his feet. Bukowski's style and content back then was sometimes likened to Lenny Bruce's high-strung, strung-out prodigal son, world-weary, raunchy wit and grit.

On that May 1975, night, the young Marines hadn't liked Bukowski's serious, philosophical poetry, the Celine-ironic, surreal existentialism he felt like reading—in a depressed mood because his girlfriend Linda King had just left him again. "Read your *good* shit!" the biggest, mouthiest of the Marines yelled.

But Bukowski held his own, was having a good timed drinking because the management had humorously, generously placed on the stage an old Frigidaire packed full of Bukowski's favorite German beer. A laugh-making prop, the fridge arm's distance close so Bukowski could reach for a beer whenever the one he was chugging was empty. When he did, the standing-room only crowd roared with delight. Bukowski's pilsner runneth over while he joked amicably, paternally with the young jar-headed Marines, told them how good they had it now that Vietnam was over. Told them they'd helped win the war over there. They cheered at that schmoozy hyperbole. *"Semper fi!"* Bukowski shouted the abbreviation of the Marine Corps motto *Semper Fidelis*, making the microphone rattle and roar. The Marines roared back.

"Hey, bartender—" Bukowski yelled. "—bring these Marines more drinks, on—" Bukowski did not offer to pay for the drinks; instead he pointed at one of the Marines, the biggest one, the mouthiest of the hecklers who'd heckled him and said: "—on *him!*

Harharharrrr!" The Marines roared some more, semper fine and mellowed, won over in the Heckle War. Booed, no more. Shut up and let Bukowski read on. Bukowski knew how to keep control and had the genius knack to make his audience happy—he let them be co-stars of his show. Plus he had his new love poems, one titled "Kiss Me" he'd written about him and Linda King published in *Wormwood Review:60* that would appear in his 1977 Black Sparrow edition *Love Is A Dog From Hell.*

"...kiss me like you've kissed all the guys I haven't heard about lately—guys under piers, at dances, on horseback, in pool halls and bowling alleys, in Mercedes-Benzes, in closets, waiting rooms, madhouses and gas stations..."

(In the spring of 1975, Bukowski had recommended I send some of my poetry to *Wormwood Review* editor Marvin Malone, who had just accepted three of my poems, which would appear in *Wormwood Review:68;* Billy Collins, who served as U.S. Poet Laureate from 2001-2003, appeared in the same publication. The issue also featured my benefactor Leo Mailman, editor of *Maelstrom Review* and *Nausea,* who in 1973 had obtained funding at CSULB for the first two issues my small press magazine *Pearl.*)

Then Bukowski read what was always a crowd-pleaser, his hilarious "The Closing of the Topless and Bottomless Bars," with the surefire laugh-getting punch-lines: "...just got to believe those Supreme boys...just can't get it up anymore." (Bukowski wrote that poem after reading my 1974 poem "Vice," from the first draft of my go-go girl memoir, then titled, *The Crotchwatchers.*) The Marines roared, stood up tall and strong, and gave him a standing ovation. It was one of Bukowski's best readings I'd ever seen—or would ever see.

Finally, August 15, 1975, when Bukowski decided the Moulton Theatre full enough and the management would let the late-comers in for free, he walked—staggered—down the aisle, yanking on the saggy butt of his drooping corduroy pants, without waiting to be introduced by the confused mistress of ceremonies who'd looked around and asked, not meaning it for the microphone, "Where is he? Where's Charles Bukowski?"

When Charles Bukowski stepped up onto the stage carrying the remainder of his six-pack, the mistress of ceremonies looked more confused. After all, he looked like a Factotum, possibly the janitor come to mop up after a leaky faucet, someone you might need to call for a policeman to eject. When Bukowski sat his droopy-clad tush down, not an officious working-class intermeddler after all, in the red velvet Baroque throne chair, he sat tall, regal, entitled, like a king might who owned the place, shuffling a pack of typewritten papers, as the M.C. quietly, obsequiously stepped off the stage. The audience, the ones who recognized this alleged hired help, presumed reprobate as the featured—and famous—poet Charles Bukowski, clapped politely, apprehensively.

Bukowski waved for them to stop. Then, also apprehensive, he began to read his "subtle stuff"—as he called it—the stuff that sounded "more poetic." Poems with a romantic flourish similar to the work of Robinson Jeffers, with an Ernest Hemingway narrative reality—two writers whom Bukowski read and greatly admired and emulated in his early days.

"Read 'The Closing of the Topless and Bottomless Bars,'" I'd requested of Bukowski before he went onto the stage.

"No, no, kid. This crowd wouldn't get that poem. There aren't any topless or bottomless bars in Laguna Beach. Like I told you, Richard Nixon lives around here. Besides, I didn't bring it with me."

"But you know it by heart," I reminded him. "I saw you read it at the Golden Bear last May."

"No, kid, I won't be reading any of my Real Stuff."

He meant his vignette, Runyonesque poems about the crazy men and women he'd known on Skid Row, met at the racetracks and scruffy bars. Nor would he read his screams-from-the-balcony poems about his women—making love, lust, and war with them. Nor would he read poems with four-letter words; Lenny Bruce got thrown in jail for his blue material—and an arrest might happen here, too, in conservative Laguna Beach. He had a handful of new poems, most of which would soon be published in *Wormwood*. He was so prolific; he seldom read the same poem twice at any of his readings.

So, Bukowski was Being Good, reading philosophical poems—and the audience responded mildly, if at all. Soon Bukowski began to feel the tension in the theatre and he got tense, too. His recitation lacked flamboyance—and fun. His usual nasal, playful sotto voce and falsettos sounded contrived, uninspired, mundane, monotonal—and worse...

"Uh oh. Bukowki's bored," Linda King said to me. "Bukowski's dangerous when he's bored."

Often, for comic relief and to give himself a break from the pressure of a difficult audience, Bukowski'd pause, take an on-stage intermission, chat with the audience, break the ice, which would unleash a flood of questions—and often praise. "We love you!" a group might shout out, starting a barrage of accolades and requests for favorite poems. That night, I'd asked Bukowski to read one of my favorites, "Law," which he'd read in the 1972 Taylor Hackford documentary, a poem that ends: "...well, all right, then, let's get on with it." Another favorite that I'd asked for at that 1975 reading was his "True Story" from Steve Richmond's infamous 1965-printed Earth Rose tabloid *Fuck Hate* about a self-mutilating lover cutting off his own genitalia to please his harridan woman. Richmond was arrested for obscenity, but later exonerated in a famous court trial.

In that small Moulton Theatre arena, however, filled with the well-bred, well-fed, and obviously uptight suburbanites emitting conspicuous smatterings of coughs, uptight throats being cleared, amidst the static emptiness of No Good Vibes, as if caught amongst the ellipses of a bad review, Bukowski frowned, clicked open another beer and chugged the entire contents gone. Finally the Hanoi Jane Fonda-shag-hairdo'd woman sitting in the front row, arm's length from Bukowski's shoe, aborted the proverbial Pregnant Pause when she shouted out:

"Why are all your poems about *yourself?*"

"What do *you* write about?" Bukowski fired back, sly to answer a question with a question.

"I don't write," she sneered.

Silence. Bukowski shrugged. He had not smiled once during the reading. Bukowski without a smile on his face was like a dark day with a tornado on the way. He lit a cigarette. "Any more questions?" he asked and puffed hard to catch the flame on the match. "I'm ready for you tonight," he said, a good-natured warning, then finally, he half-smiled, finally drunk enough to see the angst of it all, get jolly over the absurdity of these readings. He was beginning to hate readings and vowed each time this reading would be his last. His finale came in 1980, at the Sweetwater Club in Redondo Beach, California, where he'd read poetry in public for the last time, though he'd keep writing for fourteen more years until his death, March 9, 1994.

August 15, 1975, Linda King sighed a sigh of relief. "Thank God, he's mellowing out." When a hostile audience irritated Bukowski, he would tell them to go get fucked and walk off the stage. He sometimes spit on people in the audience. Once he urinated into an empty wine bottle and pretended to pour it on someone who'd heckled him.

Another question from the Angry Young Feminist: "Would *you* come to hear Charles Bukowski read poems about himself?"

"I wouldn't waste my time," Bukowski said, watching his cigarette smoke snake dance, blowing around his face in the wind from the overhead air conditioner. From the audience came some ironic laughter, some deep-chested male guffaws.

"Why don't you write poems about your mother?" another feminist asked.

"My mother died of cancer when she was three."

No laughter.

"Why do you always use dirty words?" asked the Billie Jean King lookalike.

"Give me an example of a dirty word," he said.

Silence. No laughter. Everyone was so soporifically serious that afternoon. As if they had dozed off, Siesta Time. Bukowski opened yet another beer, his penultimate can, and chugged it down, staring at the ceiling, as if to say, "Fuck 'em."

"Is there any word you find offensive?" the frizzy-haired woman asked.

"*Love!*" he bellowed, breathing it into the microphone, making the word rattle *Luuuuuuv*—!"

Nervous laughter.

Then Linda King, the helpmate she often was at his readings when they got dismal or down-and-dirty, hollered, in her lighthearted Utah, down-home, home-girl drawl: "Then why are you always tellin' me you love me, Bukowski?"

Honest laughter—and loud. Finally. Some scatterings of applause. They were warming up to him. When they turned to look at Linda King in the dark back row, she waved at them and smiled big.

A cross between an Annie Oakley and Aphrodite, Linda King that night wore a sexpot-teaser mini skirt that showed off her long, athletic legs. Bukowski was a Leg Man. Linda King, in her early thirties then, loved being part of the Bukowski Show. An able, giddy sidekick in the call-and-response shtick they often performed when reading together, the vivacious, voluptuous Linda King also shined as a solo act, was as much an entertaining poet as Bukowski.

I'd just seen Linda read in July on the bill with Diane Wakoski, who'd read from her fabulous-feminist book *Dancing On The Grave Of A Son Of A Bitch* at the Laguna Beach Unitarian Church, where Linda King, flinging her long, thick, curly hair around up on the stage, a la groovy go-go girl—wiggled and giggled to her feisty, feel-good poem recently in *Wormwood Review:60*: "I feel good...ooooohhhh I just feel good all inside...like bees buzzzzz... flapp'en my wings jump'en up and down...and you ain't even going to like this poem it's just *too good*..." The previous January (1974), Linda King had enacted on stage the female's response to Bukowski's two-character poem "The Kiss," when she and Bukowski had read at California State University Long Beach: "...kiss me, she said, like you've kissed all the whores in the world...mmm, she said, that's good...we've really been fucking around too much."

At the Laguna reading, a young baritonal male heckler sounded out: "Who's your whore this week, Bukowski?"

Bukowski pretended to ponder, scrunched his pockmarked face to look like a wad of newspaper. Then, like W.C. Fields outsmarting another sucker, Bukowski replied—sounding like a cross between the comedian and a parish priest: "Ahhhhmmm, I don't know any whores." The Feminists, the Women's Libbers in the front row should've fallen in love with Bukowski for the genuine sweetness of that revelation—Bukowski really loved Women; Women were always his Main Muses, his loving leitmotifs—but those tough-cookie feminists, unforgiving of dirty deeds perped by Other Male

Chauvinist Pig Men, were indifferent to Charles Bukowski's warm praise of chaste womankind. Then he became indifferent to them. He belched into the microphone, fed up once and for all at trying to be nice. Abruptly, predictably unpredictable, Bukowski let it all hang out with—

"Man, I gotta piss," he said, seriously, then stood up and set his beer can—like a cockroach in a king's kitchen—onto the seat of the red velvet Baroque throne chair and staggered off the stage down the aisle and out to the men's room in the lobby of the Moulton Theatre—people grumbling, whispering or giggling at Bukowski's bad, super-bad manners. While he was gone, half the people in the audience left—most of them white- or gray-haired—one, an art patron, my former professor at CSULB; and, of course, leaving the lascivious scene: the entire front row of the women's libbers, the fractious, fed-up feminists.

Back from the men's room, his butt plopped back onto his red-velvet throne, Bukowski sank deeply into it as if embracing an old friend: "Man, that felt gooooood." Then he laughed, sincerely happy for the first time during this difficult reading that looked as if it were getting better now that the offended women's libbers were gone and his fans, admirers, and avid readers had moved forward to fill up the vacant front-row seats the feminists had left behind. Miscreants, heretics, and naysayers begone from the king's domain the day before his fifty-fifth birthday, twelve years before he'd become world famous for writing the movie *Barfly* and spend his sixty-seventh birthday with celebs born on August 16, too—Madonna and Sean Penn (well, August 17, but close enough)—Charles Bukowski rattled like a golden scepter his handful of paper poems and roared into the microphone, "All right! Let's get on with it, then— I'm out of beer!" Har-har-har, he laughed and the entire audience, glad to be there, laughed with him.

"This next poem I'm gonna read, from memory, is for whatser-name out there who requested it: 'The Closing of the Topless and Bottomless Bars'—" And every one from the front row to the very dark back corner of the Moulton Theatre applauded so loudly that echoes bounced off the stucco walls, as thunderously as an impending earthquake—all the Bukowski poetry lovers there that bright blue afternoon obviously liking that poem as much as I did.

After the Moulton Theatre reading, Bukowski had been invited by a group of broadminded, liberal ladies of a local Laguna Beach church to be Guest of Honor at a 6:00 p.m. fundraiser tea—finger sandwiches, cookies, no alcohol—a real tea. Any Bukowski fan with the least bit of imagination can envision how he expressed his great and grave reluctance to attend this teetotaling event. Which he didn't. I drove him to the church on time in my white VW Bug, with Linda King following in her yellow VW, his highness in the front passenger seat, his head hanging out the window.

When he saw the nice, do-good church ladies and gentlemen dressed in their Sunday-go-to-meeting clothes squinting into the sun, standing on the neat-green, newly mown church front lawn, awaiting the arrival of the famous poet amongst the church gardens abloom with flaming bougainvillea, bright blue and gold Bird of Paradise plants, pink geraniums and gardenias and yellow daisies amongst the religious icons, none of them recognizing his gargoyle face sticking out my VW Bug window, Bukowski yelled to me, "Drive on! Quick! Get me the hell away from here!" "Are you sure?" I asked. "Look at them waiting for you, Bukowski. They all want to meet you. You're a Famous Poet." "No! No!" So, not even his favorite flowers (yellow ones) could entice him, mellow him out during this yellow-orange sunsetting twilight time.

Bukowski'd had it, he'd o.d.'d on the loud—and laud—and he needed an antidote that did not include tea and cookies. So, in spite of his swelling guilt (they'd prepaid him a hundred dollars—but he'd give it back), he told me to stop at the nearest liquor store, where he bought two six-packs of cheap beer and I bought a gallon jug of cheap Chianti, and we all drove to Santa Ana to my girlfriend Suzi Q's house who fixed us all a big spaghetti dinner and baked Bukowski a chocolate layer cake which cooled and was frosted just a bit past midnight—Charles Bukowski's fifty-fifty birthday— and we all merrily sang Happy Birthday and drank cheap beer and wine and talked and harharhar'd till the dawn's early light of August 16, 1975.

The preceding italicized portion, as a poem titled "Beercan in the Garden," was published 2009 in the *New York Quarterly* and reprinted on October 11, 2012 in the *San Diego Reader*.

Charles Bukowski and Linda King, 1973

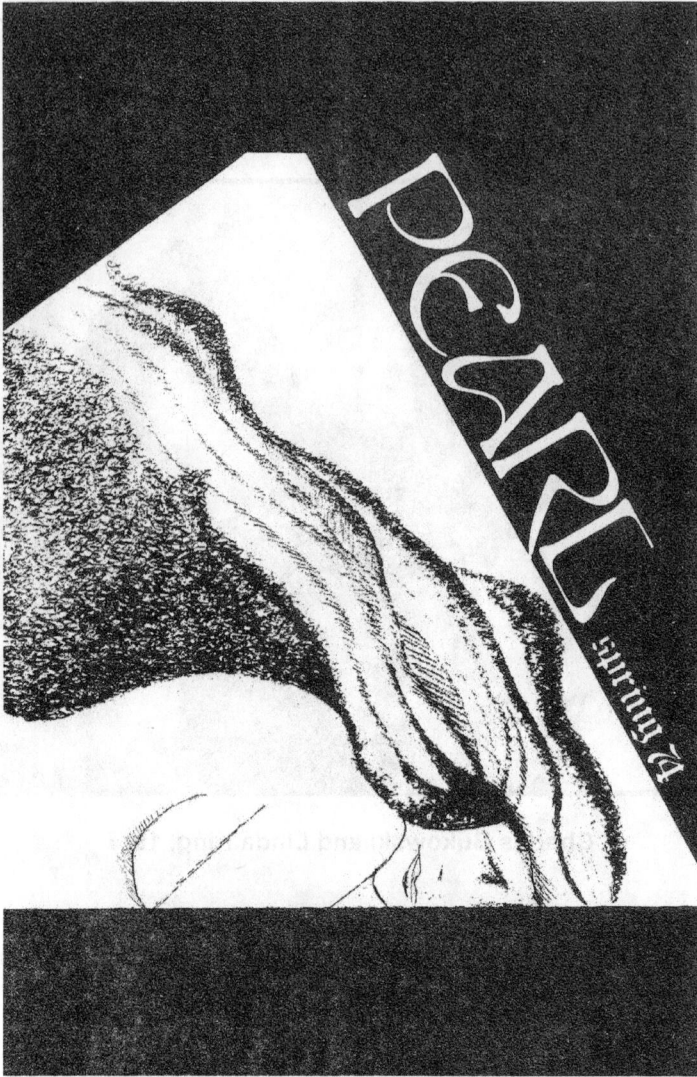

Cover of the first issue of *Pearl* (Spring 1974)—the literary magazine I founded while an undergrad at California State University Long Beach—funded by the university's Honors Program. The cover featured David Scott's logo and my artwork.

EMPTY BEER CANS & JOCKEY SHORTS
BY CHUCK BELCHOUTSKI

Reminiscence by Joan Jobe Smith

THE "SLIMIEST OF SLIME WAYS"—CHARLES BUKOWSKI WROTE me in 1974, complaining about "some prof reviewing [his] work and completely misquoting lines from poems and putting them in quotation marks to prove his point. "It disturbs like crumbs in the sheets."

Bukowski could "take the hacks," he wrote, "as long as they don't confiscate my typing machine," summing up with: "I will endure," and then assuring me that "Empty Beer Cans & Jockey Shorts by Chuck Belchoutski," a parody I'd written in 1973 after reading Bukowski's *Erections, Ejaculations, Exhibitions and General Tales of Ordinary Madness* didn't "piss [him] off." Yep, he could "take the hacks," all right. He proved that by not calling my stupid satire a piece of slime—or stupid. Which it was.

Back in 1974, just as many insecure, amateur newbie writers—those Love Dogs From Show & Tell—often do after meeting a famous genius writer, I shamelessly, uncontrollably compulsively, and opportunistically danced the "Newbie Nuzzle" with Charles Bukowski. So glad and grateful he didn't think me a bimbo, I immediately barraged him with my poetry. Sent him a rough draft of my proposed thesis for a master's degree at California State University Long Beach. (He was as disappointed as I was when they rejected *Charles Bukowski: The Poet As Entertainer*. Bukowski had looked forward to helping me write it.)

When my first issue of *Pearl* (Spring 1974) came out, I sent Bukowski a copy. Summer 1974, Bukowski's then-longtime girlfriend Linda King—the First Linda—started a mimeographed small press new little mag she named *Purr*—either an homage or hit on my first issue of *Pearl*, where I'd published her work. For her *Purr*, she'd accepted some of my poems but rejected "as being too negative and bitter" my cartoons "Mr. & MSery" about my crazy, crummy, and ever-crumbling marriage to my third husband, "T.J. DuRong."

I met Linda King first—minutes before I would meet and shake hands with Charles Bukowski—after their January 1974 co-reading at CSULB. Linda King, then thirty-three, an affable extrovert, a practicing voluptuary, her wavy hair full and shoulder-length, neared the full-bloom of her extraordinary and classical natural beauty.

That winter night, Linda King had wowed the standing-room audience of students, profs, and Bukowski fans with her own ultra-feminine, freewheeling, feisty, fun-loving poetry. Her hilarious "Green Jell-O" prose poem (one of my all-time favorite poems by any poet, dead or alive) about her and Bukowski, giddy and drunk on pure passion, pouring four boxes of green Jell-O into a bathtub to take a hot green-water bath together—both of them dyed green as a result—received loud laughs and thunderous applause as she punch-lined the supposedly erotic side effects of their green snafu: the verdant shade of the preposterous pointing part of Bukowski's genitalia and the fact that it didn't become flesh-toned again for days.

The gregarious-garrulous Linda King and I hit it off, became instant friends on the spot and still are after all these decades. I regret to this day not buying for only three dollars an autographed copy of Linda King's and Buk's collaboration *Your and My Sometimes Love Poems* published in 1972 by John Bennett's Vagabond Press. That January 1974, Linda King and Bukowski had reconciled after several weeks of separation and were *in love again*. (Their love affair would flop and flourish until November 1975). Otherwise, I would've sent her a copy of "Empty Beer Cans and Jockey Shorts by Chuck Belchoutski," which I'd written for us to have a two-sisters-cackling-feminist-witch laugh over my parody of Bukowski's Henry Chinaski, the chauvinist macho pig Chinaski, as I amateurishly first perceived Buk's prose persona—as Linda King, a self-proclaimed and proud-and-loud-about-it women's libber often saw Chinaski.

In my parody, written when I was plain old Joan Smith, I'd included the sham-shenanigan short-short story "Empty Beer Cans and Jockey Shorts by Chuck Belchoutski" in a ditto-master publication of a pretend little 'zine—with a made-up editor named Lego Jack Milkman—I'd titled *Vomit One: The one & only, 1974.* My intent: a scathing satire of *Nausea,* a small press literary journal that my future benefactor (and dear friend) Leo J. Mailman would publish for ten years in Long Beach, California, until he'd move back to Maine with his wife Barbara (whose mother was actress Ann Blyth, whose birthday was the same as Bukowski's—August 16) and their three small children. (Leo would die young in 1992 of ALS.)

My *Vomit One's* faux contributors had names like Luv-tah Pinchya, an exchange student from Eatingopiate. Some others: Buster Balls, Peter Cox, Dick Better, and the Token Woman with her poem "I Love Cock" by Lorelei Easylay, an inmate at the Metropolitan State Hospital in Norwalk, California.

But the unflappable Leo Mailman (who'd find CSULB funding for my Spring 1974 first issue of *Pearl*) thought Lego Jack Milkman and *Vomit One* hilarious and countered with, "Imitation is the highest form of flattery." *Vomit One,* my one and only foray into ball-busting feminism and women's liberation, my vengeful attempt to put male chauvinist pigdom in its yucky-mud place and shove misogyny back where the lights don't shine, had backfired. I'd failed to get the self-righteous respect I'd aimed for—receiving only laughs. Even the toothpick in a martini olive could impale and maim more painfully than my not very sword-like or mighty parody pen. Nor did I have more words-per-minute womanpower in my IBM Selectric than quantitative Charles Bukowski had hunt-and-pecking on his manual typer because Bukowski's mild reaction to my attempt at "slime ways" had been a mere question:

"Do you think ezra pound was a male chauv pig?" I had no idea in spring 1974 what or who Ezra was—I hadn't yet read him—or T.S Eliot.

What originally had triggered my itchy-witch-feminist trigger finger and wish to "confiscate his typing machine" had been the first time I'd seen Charles Bukowski read his poetry and prose, that fall 1973 at CSULB. I couldn't believe my eyes when he staggered onto the stage carrying a sheaf of typewritten papers and a brown paper sack containing a bottle filled with orange juice and vodka. Next, I couldn't believe my ears when Bukowski chug-slurped from it, then boom-belched into the microphone, and then, as if nothing cruddy had happened, he nonchalantly read new poems aimed for future publication by Black Sparrow and profane posterity in *Factotum* and *Love Is a Dog From Hell*— one a vivid depiction of a blowjob.

Pre-Buk reading that afternoon, my first poetry workshop prof, Dr. Richard E. Lee, had warned us newbie wannabe poets about that night's reading.

"Charles Bukowski is very unusual and controversial," Dr. Lee grossly understated. "There's never been an American poet like Charles Bukowski." Dr. Lee chuckled, impishly, right on bull's-eye target with that critique.

I was a newbie lit major, having first studied science to acquire admission to conventional nursing school but then changed my major. The only poetry I'd read up till then had been the usual stuff from high school—Elizabeth Barrett Browning and Edgar Allen Poe. I hadn't even read Sylvia Plath. Or Henry Miller. Anaïs Nin— of the lit-stun of Erica Jong's "zipless fuck" in her recent best seller *Fear of Flying* I'd read that following summer.

But I wasn't a newbie about life, so I thought, because I'd been a go-go girl for seven years in the mid-1960s to early 1970s and had met a lot of drunks and lechers—plus had had three rotten husbands. Furthermore, I'd just seen the porn movie *Deep Throat*, summer 1973, and thought I'd seen and heard it all until I saw Charles Bukowski, that is, in October 1973, when I heard him read lines such as: ...*love dries up... faster than sperm,* and *"I LOVE YOU!" she said./ "thanks," I said./ "Is that all you've got to say?"/ "yes."/ "eat shit!" she said and hung up.*

And then when Charles Bukowski read "...she sucked my cock/and pulled away...I rolled on top of her/stuck it in/worked it/worked it/and came...and I thought/one more fuck/I'll be even." The entire front row filled with women booed—obviously feminists—and then stood up in tandem, hardboiled soldiers, and marched down the aisle and out of the university theatre packed with standing room only.

And I agreed with those outraged females. This Charles Bukowski, this Dirty Old Man, was appalling. How could this man talk this trash? And what can I do about it? So, being a think-I-know-it-all newbie poet and an ambivalent, confused, but outraged female, I wrote an alleged scathing satire to satisfy my seething soul. And the Chuck Belchoutski-written story goes, stupidly, illiterately, like this:

> *"Sweet Jesus!" I said to myself after the doorbell had rung for half an hour. Just who in the hell could that be at my door pounding on that [bleep] of a doorbell for half an hour like some [bleep]-pounder? Oh, what did it matter, I thought, as I wrapped my hairy bod in a terrycloth newspaper left over from New Year's left lying on the floor..."*

Well, that's about all I can stand to reiterate of it. It's a hundred times worse than I remembered. I was drinking a lot of Chianti back then, that cheap Cribari. Remember it? But to further self-flagellate, teach myself another lesson, I must reiterate these pieces of Belchoutski-perpetuated trash: "My precious priapus," a girlfriend says to Chuck Belchoutski (whom I'd almost named "Chuck Upski."). But Belchoutski "pissed on her feet and laughs, then turns up the volume of the radio playing his favorite Souza march to drown out her piteous sobbing."

Thank God I only ditto'd three copies of this dumb thing. And I must now go burn the remaining copy I'd stashed away before any of my innocent bystander family members—or my good husband Fred Voss—see it and think I wrote like that for real. They may not realize its intent to be a stupid, illiterate parody because it is basically artless crap derived from emotional, subjective, ambivalent confusion rather than true objective knowledge of what Bukowski was really all about. Bukowski, one of the most original of the gritty realist writers of the 1970s parodied life, exhibiting via angst-to-ridiculous, real-to-surreal comic-socio situations, the absurdities of the perpetual but always passionate war between the sexes.

Finally, spring 1974, I had newbie-nerve enough to send Bukowski a rough draft of my true-life go-go stories, short narratives that today might be called Flash Fiction, about thirty pages that I called in 1974 *Tales of an Aging Go-Go Girl*, a title Bukowski didn't like—he said I wasn't aging, not yet. So I changed the title to The *Crotchwatchers*, which he liked. He encouraged me to write more about those days of my go-go life.

"You have really cut yourself loose into a the stratosphere. Game girl," Bukowski wrote me after reading prose poems and stories titled "Machine Cleaner," "Vice," "Nice Girls Don't," "Smitty, the Scared-Shitless Marine," "A Sack of Rotten Lunch," "Frying Pork Chops Topless," "The Crazy Ones."

But later, at University of California Irvine in 1977, my MFA mentors thought the first-person stories tawdry—and some of them really were. A 1983 rewrite, in third-person novel genre, titled *Mashed Potato Baby* was rejected by two major publishers. In 2000, after acquiring a home computer, I started all over again, this time with the apt title *Tales of an Ancient Go-Go Girl* and decided to tell my stories, my true tales, like they really were: as memoir.

I finally finished my *Tales* circa 2008. You know what happened right about then to contemporary literature: it actually flourished, as writers and wannabe writers proliferated and wrote their memoirs at the same rapid pace as bookstores and book publishers began to go broke and closed shop. Nowadays, nearly everyone is a writer, blogging, Facebooking on their magically enabling home computers that actualized, made dream-come-true the olde romantic notion that inside each human being lives a book as distinguished and unique as fingerprints, DNA, and snowflakes.

And nowadays I have many young writers, sweet Love Dogs From Show & Tell doing the Newbie Nuzzle with me. Not because I'm famous or genius but because for nearly forty years I've edited a literary journal—*Pearl*. And at this time and place a young publisher has plans to finally print my long-time-a-coming-and-a-waiting *Tales*—that old book that's been living, aging rapidly inside me for decades while I became ancient.

Maybe it'll happen. Whatever does, I owe my writing life good, bad, and tawdry to Charles Bukowski, my first mentor who pumped up my ego when he flattered me deeply in 1976 as he juxtaposed some lines he thought badly written by a famous writer by saying about mine: "On the other hand, you are contained and clean and emotional and touched with the knowledge."

Thank you, Charles Bukowski. I sure needed that then—and I, your once aging but now Ancient Love Dog From Show & Tell—always will.

What you wrote me may not be exactly true to some lit-crits out there, but your kind words I took for sure thing back then sure kept me going. But to where? Who knows until, if, and when I finally get there.

> *...some people tell me that I'm famous.*
> *what am I doing alone*
> *drunk and writing poems at 3:18 a.m.?...*
> *relentless...unheroic.*
> **–Charles Bukowski**

Illustration by Henry Denander

BUKOWSKI CHUGS CHEAP BEER @ THE NO-NO À GO-GO

Poem by Joan Jobe Smith

Bukowski laughed har har har when I told him I'd
been a go-go girl for 7 years, the bad luck time for
breaking a mirror, minimum sentence for a felony
conviction. In 1973 Bukowski'd thought me one of
those feminists who wanted to kick his ass, booed,
stomped en masse out of his poetry readings. Worse,
he'd thought me another bored housewife going back to
college, my hard working schmuck hubby buying my
books, tuition and bellbottoms, cooking his own supper,
diapering the baby while I read Sexton, Plath and Jong
and flirted with cute professors. Bukowski never drank
at any of those go-go bars I worked those 7 years. Too
expensive, too uppity and all that rock 'n' roll too noisy.
No, he preferred the bossa nova and cheap beer at the
No-No à Go-Go's where barmaids wore overalls, not
fringed bikinis and could toss out any drunk, including
him, with one bare hand. Midnights Buk phoned me long
distance, drunk because his Woman had left him again,
he listened intently to my go-go girl tales about men like
him, broke, lonely who drank too much, said wild things,
talk of men not like him: astronauts, murderers, rich men
wearing diamond pinky rings while Bukowski chugged his
cheap beer in his cheap apartment in L.A., blew smoke
from cheap cigars into the telephone at me sipping cheap
white wine 40 miles away till one night Bukowski finally
said: You gotta write about all that madness, kid. So I did.

No Va-Va-Voom Goddess

"You don't learn oomph. You are born with oomph."
—Maria Ouspenskaya, *Dance Girl, Dance*, 1940

Poem by Joan Jobe Smith

Merely an ancient go-go girl of Yore, I am always
flattered when someone thinks I was once a Stripper
capable of the extraordinary talent of strutting stuff
dancing backbends, hugging poles, caressing *baba*
au rhum goddess bod with oomph, feather boas, 7 veils
or black lace thong before tossed in the air so men hoot
More! These days I must explain what go-go meant
back then when I was a goofy fringed-bikini-clad girl
dancing not a va-va-voom but the Mashed Potato, the
James Brown, clunky Funky Chicken, Jerk, Pony or the
Monkey, some of the silliest dances ever done while
Strippers have real talent, know well how to tempt and
torture men to the furthest horizons of their endurable
anguish. Any girl in 1965 could've been a go-go girl—
if she wanted to make her parents ashamed, could shake
a tail feather without falling off the stage, never quit in
the middle of the shift to run away in tears when drunk
guys told dirty jokes—You, the punch line. Go-go side
effects hardest to bear: the smoke, beer stench foam,
jukebox blasting Mick Jagger nagging 8 days a week
what a Stupid Girl you were and vice officers who'd
arrest you for the least little sexy move—just because
bellybuttons were banned on California State beaches.
Suzi Q busted for obscenity when she did a mock bump
and grind to "Wooly Bully," got a $500 fine plus one-
year probation. My father disowned me when he found
out I'd been ratting my hair and wearing mini skirts like
Ann-Margret and he'd nearly die of shame when he drove
by Abner's 5 and saw my VW in the parking lot. Wish
he'd lived long enough to know how I had not been born
with oomph to va-va-voom and how silly go-go was so
I could've begged his forgiveness for being so untalented.

Maria Ouspenskaya in *Dance,Girl, Dance* **(1940)**

**"Joanie Gentry" @The Playgirl Club,
Garden Grove, California, 1969**

SGT. PEPPER'S
LONELY HEARTS CLUB BAND

Poem by Joan Jobe Smith

It's hard to believe today how bellybuttons
once drove men crazy in 1965, bellybuttons
the raison d'être, Original Sin of go-go bars
when French bikinis were still banned on
California state beaches and American tv
and I wouldn't wear a bikini at first, I just
wore leotards or costumes showing just a bit
of midriff, the go-go bar owners not caring,
a shy new go-go girl gave the place class, but it
drove the guys crazy, one guy one day offering me
$20 to show him my bellybutton and I told him
No, I don't have one, but he didn't believe me.
I'm a Martian, I told him, but he didn't believe
that either, he just got drunker and drunker
and yelled at me all afternoon, Hey, Baby,
lemme see yer bellybutton Baby but I kept on saying
No.
It's all so silly nowadays.
I sure could've used that $20 back then in 1965.
I still could.

Jim Morrison (The Doors, 1967)

WHISKEY À GO-GO SLOW MO WITH JIM MORRISON

Poem by Joan Jobe Smith

Whisky à Go-Go in 1965 packed in the sin and in crowd,
Brando, Warhol, Frank and Mia, me high in the corner cage
smoke in my eyes auditioning to the new band The Doors.
Stupid name said another go-go girl, lead singer always stoned
LSD-corroded croaking "Light my fie-yarrr" over and over
till blisters on our dancing feet began to bleed and we got so
tired we had to dance bugaloo slo mo so I turned down the
Whiskey job, walked to my car through Sunset Strip, Sonny
and Cher lookalikes, runaway girls, panhandling hippies,
stalled traffic and worried cops, turned right to find my VW
parked up a Hollywood hill a mile away. I cared not about this
hipster counterculture, the yeah-yeah generation outa sight cool
cats screaming Bummer, man! when narcs busted them for
possession and vagrancy or worse. Went to work at The Fort
a beer bottle's throw from the L.A. Harbor and oil refineries
packed with the working stiff sin and in crowd, stevedores, crazy
bikers, sailors, machinists who dive bombed into beer pitchers 8
days a week and left dirty screws on my tip trays instead of
dollars. The August night of the 1965 Watts riots I stood on
top the roof of The Fort a tarpaper flat the size of 50 pool tables
where guys in the band partied during breaks. I watched the L.A.
sky glow orange neon fie-yarrr, black smoke cringe crow-slap
moustaches and pierce the sunset a Van Gogh last earth dream.
As gunshots cracked and sirens screamed, I knew right then as I
read another indelible page of an unfolding starry, scary night,
that the book of my life would never be titled The Good Old Days.
But at least I'd have slo-mo shadow memories of dancing upon
the Whisky à Go-Go stage with Jim Morrison, and though a dirty
dive, The Fort was close to home and the parking space was free.

THE FORT: CONCERT BAL TOUS LES SOIRS

Poem by Joan Jobe Smith

Even I, who'd only been in the one beer bar
I'd worked so far knew that The Fort
was a hellhole, knew that the Norwegian
wharf rats the size of cats
who watched me in the storage room
used as a dressing room were not Disneyesque
knew that the 7-foot-tall Samoan brothers,
the bouncers, two dragons wearing hornets' nest collars
who smacked sawed-off pool sticks across their palms
itching for a fight, were not picturesque
and Carlita and the other go-go girls
with teenage-made gang tattoos on their hands
and rumps who stole my tips were not black comedy
but from the netherworld of mirthlessness.
The Fort, a beer bottle's throw away from
the L.A. Harbor was the kind of dive
you see in 1940s B movies where
the bad guys go to hire an assassin
the kind of place where even Genghis
and his horde would've sat
with their backs against the walls
and Crazy Ted, a Navy vet of two Big Wars
who'd received two Purple Hearts
who'd been knifed in dives from Pearl Harbor to Seoul
and crazy to boot, knew that The Fort
was the worst dive of them all because when
he walked in he rolled his eyes, pulled up
the collar of his Navy pea coat to hide his clenching jaws
and then as he sipped his beer, frowning
as if it were poisoned, he told me
Get the hell out of this place before it's too late
and while I was on the stage dancing the Temptation Walk
Crazy Ted snuck out, even though he always carried a gun.

And that night I quit
but not because of the screws that meant the obvious
some of the Bikers left on my tip trays
and not because of the drunken German sailor
who was out to get me
because he thought I stole his last dollar
and not because of the carload of Mexicans
who waited for me down the road after work
and sang "La Bamba" and yelled "PUTA!"
out the windows of their rattletrap car
while they followed me to my freeway on-ramp
nor because of the gunshots I heard every night
coming from the railroad yard across from The Fort
nor because of the lumps on the side of the road
I saw every night and was sure were corpses
nor because of the evaporating dream
of getting rich quick as a go-go girl
working double shifts
but because
I missed my three kids.

ARETHA FRANKLIN, BABY, WITH RESPECT

Poem by Joan Jobe Smith

Aretha Franklin, baby, am remembering you When.
Not that When when you wore that big hat at Obama's
Inauguration but the When of August 1966, year after
the Watts Riots when I met you at that blacks-only club
on Crenshaw in Watts week before your "Respect" aired
all over the radio and got you rich, famous and respected.
They didn't know why white chick me was in the club,
that I'd been dumped by my sexpot go-go girlfriend
Linda Alura who'd taken off with her Black Panther
lover and I didn't even drink, just sat there on the floor
on those crash pillows, snapping my white chick fingers
to the soul sound beat as you, Aretha Franklin, baby,
sang your R-E-S-P-E-C-T spelling it the way it should be
loud and clear while that groovy black dude taught me
how to Bugaloo, Shingaling, Jerk and Temptation Walk.
Oh, baby, what a rough 1966 I had while you moved on
to a great future. My 1967 wasn't much better so when I
auditioned at the Condor Room up in North Beach, I
picked on the jukebox for irony and good luck your new
hit song Respect, just a little bit of respect I wanted, too,
in those days when just a gaudy go-go girl. I got the job
but turned it down, too scared to go topless, so came back
to L.A. go-go. And now, Aretha Franklin, baby, you're
not doing well; news of your illness got me remembering
you, though you'll never know how much I respect you,
remember every day your soul sound real and wise, your
black woman big heart, your finger-snappy upbeat always
got me going when it was my turn to dance, even when I
didn't want to—but always remembering how to spell
R-E-S-P-E-C-T right and proud when no one else did.

Aretha Franklin, 1968

FEMINIST ARM CANDY
FOR THE MAFIA & FRANK SINATRA

Poem by Joan Jobe Smith

Go-go girl Sindy, who changed the first letter of her name
from "C" to "S" for obvious reasons, said us go-go girls
at the Playgirl Club in 1968 were nothing but waitresses
in bikinis, dancing workhorses, indentured servitude (she
forgot to mention how much money we made, more than
tenured Cal Tech profs, aerospace executive engineers, we
drove new cars, dressed groovy as Cher, had cuter boyfriends,
guys in the band were *our* groupies). So Sindy decided to
organize a Go-go Girl Union, make our millionaire bosses
give us lunchtime, sick leave, retirement funds, vacation pay,
overtime for that hour extra we worked cleaning up the place
while our mean boss Spike called us lazy tramps. Sindy went
to the California state labor board, ACLU, wrote letters to our
Congressman detailing us go-go girls's "UNendowment of
inalienable Rights" promised us in the U.S. Constitution and
when the bosses told her Shut up, get back to work, one night
she shing-a-linged, right in the middle of Dick Dale's famous
showstopper solo, Sindy jumped off the stage, pulled the plug
on Dick Dale's electric guitar—rrrip!—as off she went to Vegas
for some fun in the sun, be a showgirl at the Stardust or Flamingo,
find a millionaire to marry and 6 months later when she returned
to hello-goodbye-again, 20 pounds thinner, hair bleached white
dried-up Monet haystack, eyes swollen from a day-ago beating,
nostrils cracked from snorting cocaine, eyeballs red from day-
time pot smoking and a slipped disc because they'd made her
wear 50-pound headpieces, work 8 days a week plus matinees
and be arm candy after hours for the Mafia and Frank Sinatra,
she warned us: "Stay the hell away from Vegas, baby, the men
are very BAD there." Then Sindy walked out, the first feminist
go-go girl, off again this time for Chicago, her name changed
to Windy as in bad weather blowing in. What Windy would do
there in the Windy City of Chicago to make the world right for us
go-go girls and women everywhere to find Life, Liberty and the
Pursuit of Happiness in turn-on, tune-out 1969, God only knew.

King of the Surf Guitar—Dick Dale, 1960s.

GO-GO GIRL REUNION

Poem by Joan Jobe Smith

Those who don't show up at Reunions either
think they're too good or have something to hide.
So since go-go girls once let it all hang out of bikinis
and can claim neither that vice nor the virtue, we all
showed up at the Playgirl Club where 10 years before
we'd all slung beer and shook our tail feathers till 2 a.m.
Jenny the most beautiful and best dancer of all was there
wearing pink shantung and a sable, the only one of us
to marry a millionaire although we all tried and Jodi
showed up, now thinner and a reborn Christian; Tiara,
too, in spite of warrants for her arrest. Barbie was still
a barmaid but now lived with a younger, better-shooting
pool hustler; Linda Lee just bought a new Mercedes, a
nose job and boob job all paid for by one of her old sugar
daddies. And Dee-Dee, wearing thick glasses, her eyes
having gone bad from too much LSD, had kicked drugs
and now drank nothing but Jack Daniels on the rocks.
Betty had given up macramé and now taught aerobics.
Suzi Q got a brokers license and was getting rich quick
on commercial real estate; Cher--not the real one--just got
her PhD in Psychology from Prestigious U and said she'd
seen more weirdoes and crazies when she was at the Playgirl
than she ever saw in a Psycho ward. The new Playgirl owner
Dick Dale had his band play "Night Train" and all us old go-
go girls drunk enough got up on the stage, raised skirts above
our knees and wiggled around while Dick Dale took Polaroids
and said over the microphone to the audience and us that us
go-go girls weren't getting older we were only getting better
and above the whistles, hoots and applause, I heard one of
his 20something cocktail waitress laugh to a co-worker and
say: *"Yeah, sure,"* knowing, certain that she would never
show up to any reunion of any kind. Wizened with young,
she thought she knew how to hold back sunsets with her tongue.

MENIS LIB POSTER.

BUK

THINGS GOT DIRTIER AND WORSE IN 1972

Poem by Joan Jobe Smith

When *Deep Throat* the movie showed all over Southern
California, go-go went-went, topless toppled, bottomless
bars bottomed out as priapic men became too impatient
to even watch strippers at the Pussycat so the Playgal owners
cleaned up their act to get richer, turned their go-go place
into a nite club, painted the red walls golden, got a cocktail
license to rid the stench of beer, got waitresses who wore
togas, fired the former boss, bouncers and gofers with Mafia
ties, hired blonde, red-faced Mad Dog Mike, the size of a
sunburned brick wall, a wrestling champ with an MBA who
carried a briefcase as big as a district attorney's, booked
good bands, live Vegas acts and the place became packed
with a younger generation disgusted with unkempt hippie
stuff, wanted to dress up now, wear suits, billowing skirts
and blow-dry their hair. Elton's boogie and Johnny Cash's
Texas 2-step made it sexy and cool to touch-dance again;
couples horned coke in the bathroom to sip soda till sunrise
while Mad Dog Mike took credit for the groovy scene until
one day the FBI came and shot up mirrors, winged a waitress,
busted up a gun-drug-white-slave-child-porn ring headed by
Mad Dog Mike and some badass Riverside bikers so vile
they made the Hell's Angels I knew in the 1960s seem like
lacemakers and worst of all, inside Mike's briefcase the FBI
found ingredients to make an atom bomb and in the midst of
this notoriety the Playgal owners sold the place for enough to
buy a Hawaiian island and then along came John Travolta and
disco and dancing turned solo stud time, punk rock made it all
vicious, MTV, Michael Jackson and Madonna's removable
bullet bra brought the world narcissistic crotch-watching and
just when you think things can't get worse and dirtier, they do.

Illustration by Henry Denander

"If you're a man, Los Angeles is where you hang it up and bat-tle, or if you're a woman and you've got enough leg and the rest, you sail it against a mountain backdrop so when you grow old and grey you can hide away in Beverly Hills in a mansion so nobody can see how you've decayed..."

CHARLES BUKOWSKI

OLD GO-GO GIRLS NEVER DIE

Poem by Joan Jobe Smith

—they just fray away, laughed the guys. Get it?
they'd ask, pointing to the beer-stained fraying-
away fringe on our bikinis. The guys, schaden-
freudens, liked the idea that us young girls'd
get old, fat and gray someday—hopefully soon
so they could say No to us like we did to them
and as us girls watched the times a'changin' the
go-go thing go topless, bottomless, then the wet
T-shirt contests and Pussycat porn theaters (the
future horror of female mud wrestlers and lap
dancers surpassed even our cynical imaginations),
us girls moved on, covered up our bellybuttons,
put away our frayed bikinis, crammed our bods
into business suits to stagger as shellshocked
as Vietnam vets into alarm-clocked mornings, lit-
bright coffee offices with screaming telephones,
mind-clattering typewriters instead of jukeboxes.
Old go-go girls good at math became real estate
brokers, know-it-all girls went back to college for
teaching creds. Cher (not the real one) got a PhD.
Judy G who'd dated a Righteous Brother managed
his rock 'n' roll nightclub. Nila, former President
of Dick Dale's Fan Club became his Girl Friday.
Mimi married a millionaire. But by the 21st century
they'd all disappeared. Where did all those go-go
girls go? I wanted to know. Repeat to them the old
go-go girl joke all those guys liked best: How many
go-go girls does it take to screw in a light bulb? None.
Because go-go girls screw in waterbeds. Get it? I'd
ask all the old go-go girls and they'd get it all right
and laugh ho-ho while they sip the imaginary tea I
make them right now, laced with cognac or tequila,
crystal meth or absinthe, Nyquil or Ben & Jerry's
Cherry Garcia or Botox or whatever nepenthe it
takes these days to keep girls from fraying away.

Illustration by Henry Denander

"I die a little every day. We all do."

CHARLES BUKOWSKI

SENDING SINATRA BACK TO HEAVEN

Poem by Joan Jobe Smith

Dreamed again last night I was a go-go girl
again, still thin enough to wear a bikini, toes
still tough enough to go-go dance in high heels,
my ancient bosom still push-up-able, am able
to carry two pitchers of beer in each fist even
though I haven't been able to open a jar of pickles
since 1986 but just like all those other recurring
Ancient Go-Go Girl dreams, I'm terrified knowing
how the other go-go girls and the guys in the band
and my mean Simon Legree boss Spike will all
laugh at me when they find out the Truth: that I
snuck into this go-go bar I worked in so long ago.
They'll think me a pervy old broad spying on them
in their rock-out house of cool and groovy. And
making things worse last night, Frank Sinatra
wanted to date me, come fly with him, have one
for the road after I got off work and I didn't want to,
didn't know what to do: Tell him: Hey, Frank, this
is just a dream? In real life I'm a married woman?
I'm really 700-years-old and besides, Frank, you're
DEAD! But I can't tell Frank Sinatra that; it'd make
him mad; can't tell him either we have nothing in
common: Frank's a Sagittarius and bossy. Frank'd
make me wash his socks and bake lasagnas every
day and I'm a lazy but law-abiding Aquarian and
I'd call the cops when fink he hung with the Mafia and
and then I'd have to go on the lam, hide out in a dark
room to write a poem about him like I'm doing
right now in Real Life after I woke up an hour ago,
sending Frank Sinatra back to heaven where Frank
belongs for singing all those beautiful love songs.
And then, having nothing else to do, I baked my
husband a great big vegetable lasagna and washed
his socks. I'm not so lazy after all and I'd really had
a really, really hard day's night—being young again.

Frank Sinatra, 1960s

CHARLES BUKOWSKI:
A BEER CAN IN THE GARDEN

From *Tales of An Ancient Go-Go Girl*
Memoir by Joan Jobe Smith

CHARLES BUKOWSKI SAT IN THE MOST COMFY SPOT IN MY living room, in a cavernous antique red velvet throne chair with handcarved oak armrests and claw feet, and leaned his big leonine head below where I, his liege, age thirty-five, sat on a footstool, looking up at him. Age fifty-four, slimmed down, the most handsome he'd ever be, he brushed my waist-length post-hippie hair away from my ear and, his breath hot with alcohol, whispered into it: "Six inches."

Then, on this Friday night of April 11, 1975, 7:35 p.m., four days before the hundred and tenth anniversary of the demise of Abraham Lincoln and the sixty-third anniversary of the sinking of the *Titanic*, though we were celebrating neither of those historical facts, Charles Bukowski grabbed one of the many magnums of cheap champagne I'd bought and placed to chill in a wash bucket of ice cubes on my coffee table my no-good third husband T.J.'d made from an old Victorian oak dining room table by sawing off its legs. Charles Bukowski popped open the machine-gun sized green bottle and poured us both long, gobletsful shots of the bubbly stuff because I, the hostess of this party in Charles Bukowski's honor, couldn't. Because my right thumb was broken and harnessed up in a newfangled contraption made of beige Velcro-clasped plastic and canvas, a thick and longish erect brace that made him laugh har-har and say once again because Charles Bukowski liked to repeat himself when he'd said something especially controversial, entre nous, he said it, but loud enough to set off burglar alarms on the next block: "SIX INCHES!"

"Six Inches" the title, too, of one of his raunchiest short stories. About a man, much to his horror, suddenly turning into a six-inch penis so's to forever satisfy whenever she wanted—his oversexed woman from hell. I'd never read that story, knew I didn't want to even though university profs who liked him likened it to Kafka existentialism. I wasn't much crazy about Bukowski's sexcapade fiction he'd begun writing during the mid-1960s sexual liberation, which now, during the Everything Goes Swinging Seventies, was considered by his admirers tour de force cause celebre. Secretly, I thought some of it was vulgar. Porn, even. I was especially offended by the recent story in *Hustler* he'd "written for the bucks," but I wouldn't've dared tell Bukowski. I was sort of in love with him. But don't tell anyone.

This "six inches," my broken thumb, was the reason a week ago I'd cancelled my Big Bukowski Bash to honor him, my next feature in the fourth issue of my small press magazine *Pearl* that I planned to produce with part of my next student loan which would also pay for my fall semester law school tuition. Bukowski had generously obliged my publishing entrepreneurship with a batch of unpublished poems. For the cover, he'd offered one of his Thurberesque ink drawings that he titled "Men's Lib Poster." The drawing featured a little "six-inch" man looking up the skirt of a gargantuan, voluptuous woman that bore more than a passing resemblance to me.

Thinking Bukowski would enjoy the mix of humanity at this party, I'd invited my all-male study group of seven from law school plus a bunch of poets and profs from the university I'd graduated from four months before with a B.A. in creative writing. Law and Literature. A more motley caustic crew there'd never be as the law students shot pool in the garage mumbling about "that dissolute Bukowski" and the poets, with their notebooks huddled in corners jotting and doodling, pretended to be invisible. This party would remain, along with going to law school and marrying T.J., on my Top Ten List of Things I Wish I'd Never Done.

Rescheduling the Party In His Honor so pissed off Bukowski—who wasn't used to being rescheduled—that I held it as soon as possible before I pissed him off forever and he took back his poems and "Men's Lib Poster" (he was a pretty petulant and unforgiving cuss). I held the party, even though my thumb hurt like hell, still throbbing, freshly busted just Thursday night before last, down by the Huntington Beach Pier, two doors down from The Golden Bear, a bistro where Bukowski occasionally appeared to read his raucous poetry—he was getting more and more popular among the pay-to-see crowd of young intellectuals, old hipsters, aging hippies who went there to see the likes of Crosby Stills and Nash, Joan Baez, and post-Woodstock maestros like that.

My thumb got busted at the joint when my third husband T.J. jerked loose my fist clutching his fuzzy hair I'd snatched onto after I caught him walking down Main Street happy as you please, in fact he was whistling "come on baby light my fire," arm in arm with a cute hippie chick wearing a long orange and yellow madras cloth skirt. I chased him down the alley in back of the Golden Bear then up Pacific Coast Highway where he tried to make a quick getaway in his beat up gray primer-coated 1936 Chevy pickup he'd named "The Frog" and bought a vanity license plate that said "RRIBBT" though he'd never gotten around to painting it toad green like he kept saying he was going to. But I caught the sneaky bastard before he even got behind the steering wheel because I'd outrun him—with only one shoe, too, a four-inch high-heeled wedgie at that—even though he'd been a track star in high school. So he said. My no-good third husband T.J. lied to me about everything. After eight years of marriage, he was driving me crazy. And so was the first semester of law school.

Bukowski'd warned me about law school. "Feed your brain on me," he'd said.

"When's T.J. getting home?" asked Linda King, Bukowski's beauteous sexpot of a young girlfriend after hearing the champagne blather all the way out in the garage T.J.'d converted with *Playboy* centerfold wallpaper and Budweiser beer signs to resemble a rec room (a "Frog Farm" he called it) where she'd been shooting pool with my all-male study group. That cheap California-made stuff was so carbonated, its cork pop was as loud as a whale belch. My Wandering Third Husband, that no-good T.J.'d been gone for two days and nights, obviously having forgotten this Big Bukowski Bash. He'd been looking forward to it, too, because he had a big crush on Linda King, as did most men who ever laid eyes on her. I shrugged, dunno. "Well, when he gets home, tell him Big Mama's looking for him."

"Oh, yeah?" said Bukowski.

"Yeah, Bukowski."

Linda King, the Famous Lusty Linda who'd starred for the eight years they'd been together in many of Bukowski's Women poems and would play a leading role in his book entitled *Women*, That Linda walked away, sashaying her voluptuous rear beneath her tight mini-skirt as she went, then said over her shoulder, "Don't do anything I wouldn't do, Bukowski."

Briefly, she glowered at me, pretending to be jealous, making sure Bukowski saw her doing it. Then when he bent to light up a cigar, she winked. She and I were actually good friends, talked weekly on the phone long distance, her in L.A., me in the Orange County suburbs. It was because of her, after I'd featured her, a poet in her "own write," in my first three all female issues of *Pearl*, that I'd got hooked up literarily with Bukowski. What I, an only child, liked most about the women's lib was how we women were supposed to be "sisters." I'd always wanted a sister and sometimes, because Linda was one of five sisters and well rehearsed at mingling with her own gender, she made me feel like one. And, already drunk enough on this champagne, so cheap it wasn't even worth its weight in potatoes, I glowed with being-someone's-sister pride.

"All right, baby, sure, I won't do anything *you* wouldn't do, yeah, sure," he said, sarcastically, blowing smoke into the air toward her as she walked away. Chugging the goblet of fizzy, then pouring himself and me some more, he winced, then growled: "What a long drink of piss this is. You know, don't you, men only pretend to like champagne to get into women's skirts." He looked at my starving student attire, the Levi's I wore, and shrugged. "Even Cary Grant hates champagne."

He drank the stuff anyway. Bukowski always liked to drink up the hosts' stuff first at parties in his honor (and there were many such parties back then in 1975 when he was in the process of climbing out of the Skid Row gutter to put his foot permanently and pyrotechnically onto the slippery sidewalk of American literature). When it was all gone, he'd drink what he preferred, his own BYOB—usually vodka that he carried in a brown paper sack.

Bukowski took another look at my harnessed erect broken thumb, shook his head, and har-hared again. Admiringly, you see, because when Bukowski found out why I'd cancelled the party—I'd lied at first, saying I had the flu, which was what pissed him off, the obviousness of the excuse, the phony appeal to his presumed poet humanity (of which he was in short supply and mostly saved for his poetry) to forgive my low-immune frailties—he thought *the truth*, my broken thumb, and how it happened hilarious, because it was so tawdry, and said: "I ought to put you and Linda on the bill down at the Olympic. Either of you would tear the average prelim boy to pieces. God save the male race or at least my part of it anyhow with two women like you and Linda who love their men so much!"

I didn't love that no-good T.J., and hadn't since 1972, when he started driving me crazy and to drink. And now law school was making me crazier and drink even more. Since starting law school in January, I'd gained another five pounds. It wasn't that studying law was so hard—not when you got a gift of gab and a short-term memory like mine able to cram full of useless information for final exams. And law school, unlike English and literature, my undergrad majors, made sense with its specific—though endless—lists of logical rules, laws, exceptions to the rules and laws, even the loopholes foreseeable glottal stops when compared to the unfathomable, illogical raison d'être of comma splice, homonym and 'i' before 'e' except after 'c' and much easier to remember, gentle krill in the gullet of my fat whale mind. Yet it was pure drivel. Law school a chore, a rite of passage to weed out the workhorses from the slump-backed nags because that's what being a lawyer was really all about: Work. Lots of hard, hard work. I hated it.

And I especially hated my all-male study group members, mainly the unmarried ones, out in the garage shooting pool with Linda—Kirk the Work and Facto Jacko (everyone in the group had a nickname, except for me—at least not one I knew about). When alone with them, Kirk the Work and Facto Jacko sexually harassed me. The most recent incident had occurred two weeks before when we'd studied products liability and defamation together at Jacko's cheap apartment across the street from the law school and they'd spent two hours trying to talk me into a ménage a trois, Kirk even going so far as unfastening the top button of my Levi's. "A little juris-IM-prudence," Kirk kidded me not. Finally, after not learning a thing—except a refresher about what shits men could be in 1975—I went home.

"Don't do it, baby," Bukowski had slurred one night last January after Linda had left him "for good" (yet again). He called drunk after I'd written him that I was going to law school. He said, "Law. That's a bigger mirage than *love*. A few fat manipulative cats break through the barricades to walk the greensward, but it's strictly trickery and low class. All they can concentrate on is digging in. The most vicious people that I have known, those furthest away from reality and compassion, are lawyers." And then he added, "And the college professors. And these, teach. Be careful, Joan."

Oh well. I wasn't going to be in law school much longer. I just knew it. Something was going to happen to interfere. Something unforeseeable, odd, and potentially dangerous—and not this broken thumb—was going to end my pursuit of Lawyerness. I didn't know what. But it was coming. Peeking at me with its thousand eyes from the horizon of hell.

"Mom," said my oldest daughter Leah, aged sixteen and a half. "MOM!" She was upset, nearly shouting at me, unusual for her, a soft-spoken, gentle girl, a Libra, if you believe in astrology. "Come look at this!" She narrowed her green eyes the color of her father's, my first husband, the Black Irish alcoholic, and led me down the hallway to her bedroom. "I thought your friends were all smarty pants intellectuals. College graduates. Respectable people."

That's what I'd told her about people who were educated, people I wanted her to be like, to be like me and go to college. No, she hated school, knowledge, learning "stuff." All she wanted in life was to get married and have children. I hoped she'd want to *do* something when she grew up. I hoped I was setting an example of what that could be: Lawyerdom.

"Look…" She squeaked open her bedroom door, and there was Jacko having sex with one of the women poets I'd invited, the famous L.A. one, a university Ph.D. prof and Oleander Prize recipient who'd soon marry Facto Jacko, pay his law school tuition, then after he graduates and receives his "License to Steal," as my all-male group called our future law degree, and passes the bar exam, and dumps her for his legal secretary, she'll vanish and never be heard from ever again. But, right then, they were copulating. In front of the green Black Irish eyes of my innocent, soft- spoken, sixteen-and-a-half-year-old gentle daughter in her own bed decorated with koala bear sheets and comforter in her own bedroom with matching koala bear wallpaper and curtains she'd bought with her own money working at an ice cream parlor.

"My God! You guys!" I cried before I shut the door, ashamed for them and me.

"Some example, Mom, these friends of yours, these so-called intellectuals. A bunch of pervs. They're no better than those dirt-bag biker and hippie and ex-convict friends of T.J.'s! Bukowski is a horrible man. You told me he was a genius."

"Yeah, Mom, what's the deal?" demanded Sean, my fourteen-year-old son. "What's so special about this dirty old man?" he asked, a high school innocent who'd only read one book, *The Andromeda Strain,* and did not know Bukowski had written a book titled *Notes of a Dirty Old Man.* "A genius? I don't think so. Know what he's doing right now? Peeing in a champagne bottle, Mom, and then drinking it! His *own urine!*"

Not really. I peeked down the hallway to where I could see Bukowski in the middle of the living room. He was only pretending to, trying to shock the law students giving him a bad time, gawking at him, making snide, know-it-all lawyerly remarks, things like prima facie, res ipsa loquitur, non compos mentis, all to the delight of one of the university lit profs and a couple female poets who didn't much like him, enjoyed the comeuppance they perceived. The gawking male tyro poets there who liked him didn't even seem to notice the caustic commotion because they wanted To Be Bukowski, wanted to garner this kind of attention, however provocateur, some day, any old way. Imagining themselves in Bukowski's place, they just smiled beatifically, thinking Hooray and hallelujah. You've got it coming to ya.

"Even T.J.'s never done anything so stupid. Your law school pals are all laughing at him. And laughing at you, too, for inviting him. I can't believe you, Mom, hanging around a dirty old man like him."

My kids had never talked to me like this before. Reprimanding me, their Mom, a college grad, a Junior Bar Association member on her way to a juris doctorate degree. (Maybe.) Leah and Sean stomped away to go outside to talk about my disgusting party with Linda's handsome nephew Raymond Shurtz who was Leah's age, didn't approve of the carryings-on either, all of them drinking Pepsis as they leaned on the Thing parked out front, a strange Volkswagen product du jour in which Bukowski'd been hauled by Linda who owned it all the way from L.A. to my party in the suburbs.

The party didn't get any better, even as I got drunker and drunker waiting for T.J. to come home, but who never did though Linda seemed to have a good time out in the garage dancing with the law students and poets and university profs and Bukowski, too, seemed to be having the time of his life, at least for a while flirting with my beautiful dark-haired and young girlfriends Marilyn and Kay in the living room, matching him drink for drink, while he held court from the red velvet throne chair like a king. He liked women who could hold their liquor, he said, and he liked women with good legs, eyeing up the dark crotch of Marilyn's denim midi skirt.

"What the hell?" he bellowed after getting a gander of her lacy knee-length undies. "What in the hell are those things?"

Marilyn answered in her sweet voice: "Petti-pants. Beaver Cheaters, some call them."

"Har-har! I remember those things from the sixties! Peter Cheaters I called them. My first wife wore those things! What you got underneath them? Hmmm?" His big leonine head dawdling, he was getting very drunk, he leaned forward holding a magnum champagne bottle as if it were a flashlight to brighten the darkness of her crotch, as if she would show him.

"My regular undies."

"You're wearing *two* pair of underwear? One a pair of Peter Cheaters? Christ, what a cockteaser! Take them off!" Marilyn, not a cockteaser at all, happily married twelve years to a firefighter and was also my *Pearl* co-editor said, "No way, Jose" and giggled. "Take them off!" he roared, ho-ho-ho, Santa Claus in April, shaking his big head, knocking loose some of his dark hair slicked back with pomade.

"Take what off, Bukowski?" asked Linda, who, I had come to realize had Hound of the Baskervilles ears and the ever-presence of protoplasm, sneaky and snaky as smoke—necessary attributes to keep apace with Bukowski.

Then, just as I'd heard from Linda, read about in Bukowski's many books, and seen for myself recently in Taylor Hackford's documentary *Bukowski*, their intensity contingent upon their alcohol consumption, Linda and Bukowski began to argue, loudly, and the party wasn't fun for anyone anymore. The law students had all left hours before, after they'd chowed down two two-gallon pots of homemade Joan's Own Chili, even the vegetarian one with carrots and parsnips in it they'd mistaken for chorizo. All the poets had also gone, with just Marilyn and Kay remaining, but quietly exiting, giving me little paltry waves of fearful goodbye as Linda's and Bukowski's going-on-eight-years, give-and-take, give-as-good-as-you-get, don't-go-down-without-kicking accusations and heart-crime grievances got louder.

"I am a beer can in the garden!" Bukowski proclaimed, now chugging his BYOB wrapped in a brown paper bag.

"You're a drunk asshole, Bukowski," said Linda.

He ignored her and went on.   "I'm an umlaut in Alsace-Lorraine! The first spark of the fire from the torch that burned down the Library of Alexandria!"

"You're a firebug all right, Bukowski, you scorched all my furniture with your cigars."

When she fluffed her long curly hair as a got-the-last-word gesture, Bukowski's eyes, though seeming to swirl in their sockets, gazed at her for a long moment, glistening with great affection.

As one last law student snuck out, Kirk—Linda's paramour of the night, her constant dance-and-pool partner that was supposed to be T.J.—Bukowski shouted to him: "And you, you long drink of piss –"

Standing at six feet, five inches, Kirk was nearly a head taller than the six-foot Bukowski hunkering down his head, a raging bull about to butt him in the chest.

"Don't think for one minute I don't know what you and Linda have been up to all night! I got eyes in the back of my head, too, Linda. You, you elongated wormy shyster. You ambulance chasing Shylock, I got a pound of flesh for you, all right."

Bukowski grabbed his crotch as if a sack of potatoes inside his navy blue corduroy pants had tumbled loose. Kirk jumped back in fear as if Bukowski had aimed an Uzi.

"You litigious lug nut, you are the sweaty hair on the wart of an asshole's asshole!"

Kirk shot me a dirty look between the eyes that had it been bullets would've splattered my brains all over my living room wall—and he didn't even shut the front door when he left, just ran out, fast as a track star.

"And you—You, Jooooan, Jooooan you are –"

Bukowski turned to me sitting on the floor in front of my fireplace and the croaking fire, merely the gas jet flapping heat because I could not afford logs to burn because of my astronomical law school tuition. I shivered in fear at what Bukowski thought I was. "You, you are a honeybee upon the tundra."

It would be the nicest thing he'd ever say to me except when he calls next winter after Linda leaves him following their biggest fight ever to read me a poem he will write about my nose. Bukowski liked noses, too, along with women with good legs who can drink as much as he can But then he added: "Jooooan, you're getting faaaat." He eyed, disapprovingly, my burgeoning bosom fattened up from drink. He was, after all, a Leg Man.

"And what am I, Bukowski? An ant at the picnic?"

"You, Linda, my great beauty, you are the woman of all women. You, you, Linda, Linda, you have pink and orange butterflies sewn upon your thighs." Bukowski pulled another cigar from his shirt pocket but could not light it because he was so drunk.

Finally Raymond, Linda's nephew arrived, as if SOS'd via secret telegraph wire, and helped Bukowski, bent and staggering, out the door to be driven safely back to Los Angeles in that ugly Thing all in one surly, shit-faced piece. And the party was over. Thank God. Next to law school and my three husbands, one of the biggest mistakes of my life. As I chugged the very last goblet of the cheap champagne, warm as urine—my God, was it urine?—the urine of Charles Bukowski? I sniffed it. No, it wasn't—a rumor after all—t'was just plain old cheap California champagne gone flat and caustic as sandpaper as it scraped my esophagus on its way down—look out, gums, here it comes.

I heard a shuffling of feet in the hallway. "T.J.?" I called. "You sneaky bastard! Is that you?"

"No. S'me…" said the last law student.

Yet another one. My God, they were like ants at a picnic. Yawning, stretching, it was Nicholas the Ridiculous (the only good-looker) from my study group, nicknamed that by Facto Jacko not me, called that behind his back, but called Nick the Quick to his face, again, not by me but the rest of the group, though Nick did not know that was a slur, too, referring to his flabbergasted filibustering when called on in class to summarize aloud our daily case studies, law school teaching all of us to think on our feet, which Nick was not good at—not at all, poor guy. He would flunk out with a pitiful 1.65 GPA the first semester after our June finals. I was never called on in class, the profs already pushing me to the side out of the pack, not worthy of even the humiliation of being called on, presumed a bimbo, I suspected because I'd gotten so bosomy from all my drink.

After Jacko the Facto receives a 4.0 and I tie with Kirk the Work for second highest score in Torts that June, a 3.75 that will so surprise my Torts prof, he will hold a special inquiry as to the possibility that I cheated (based upon a rumor instigated by Kirk). I will be exonerated but with much shame and implication that "where there's smoke there's fire," or: the "But for" law. No, intentional infliction of mental distress and malicious prosecution and disparagement won't be any of the reasons I won't finish law school.

Nick the Ridick yawned again, then looked around, asked: "Where's that snide prick?"

"Bukowski?"

"No. Facto Jacko. He took my car keys after I fell asleep on that couch in your dining room. Man, I'm tired, all the time tired, tired. Law school's really tough, man. Where's Jacko?" I shrugged, not knowing that at that very moment Jacko and the famous woman poet were, carpe diem, eloping to Las Vegas, Nevada, in Nick's red 1971 Datsun. "Who's Bukowski?"

"My guest of honor, Charles Bukowski, the famous poet." Nick looked confused. I tried to explain. "Bukowski, the one who sat in the red velvet chair all night in my living room."

"Famous? That pervert? That repugnant reprobate? Famous for what?"

"His amazing poetry. He's widely published. Makes a lot of money. He'll read at the Golden Bear next week. He's a poet." Nick still looked confused like that clueless, but sweet, innocent, malapropping older lady in the liquor store in Taylor Hackford's *Bukowski* documentary who, after Bukowski told her he was a Poet, asked: "Polack?"

"A poet? You're kidding, right? That debauched derelict? We all thought he was some deranged alcoholic bum you found on skid row and invited to your party. You mean to tell me people *pay* to read his poetry? Bookstore owners had better post big *caveat emptor* signs next to his books to absolve themselves of product liability. Man, what a show he put on. Your name's mud, baby. You'll be the laughingstock of law school after Kirk and Jacko get through telling everyone about this party. I'd advise you to quit law school asap."

My name really will be Mudd—as in Samuel A. Mudd, the ill-fated Good Samaritan bandager of John Wilkes Booth, Abraham Lincoln's assassin—beginning that Tuesday we all return to law school, April 15, the day the *Titanic* sunk and Abraham Lincoln died of assassin's wounds.

"Ms. Mudd"—nicknamed that by my study group members who will blackball me. But my libelous, besmirched reputation won't be the reason, either, that I don't become a lawyer. It'll be because of an Attractive Nuisance, as it's called in Torts, another party, another disastrous bash—and one even worse than my Big Bukowski Bash.

"Brrr, I'm cold," Nick said, sitting beside me on the floor to warm his feet next to the gas-jet-leaping woodless flame in the hearth.

We sighed, tired, miserable, en tandem just as T.J. walked in. My third husband. Only thirty-three years old at that moment, he'd aged five years since I'd seen him Wednesday last, his coffee- and whisky-stained handlebar moustache drooping like burnt broom straw down his chapped lips, his prematurely graying fuzzy hair sticking out like a rat's nest from his wrinkled, leather cowboy hat, gone limp and floppy as an old shoe sole from all the times he'd been caught in the rain, having to walk miles to a gas station after having a flat tire on a lonely road or from sleeping in the ditch because he'd locked his car keys inside the car. A squint line between his eyes deep as a Malibu arroyo from his many days beach-bumming in the California sun, he looked like an ancient high plains-drifting Sundance Kid who'd led a wagon train west across the Rockies, the Mojave, the Sierras and California to Honolulu via Tokyo, Japan. T.J. smelled like it, too.

"What the fuh—?!" gasped T.J., thinking he'd caught me at last in an act of turpitude after all my years of almost catching him. "Aha!" he proclaimed like a got'em-cornered Pinkerton Man, then got the most awful look of disgust on his face just as I figured out what he thought he had caught me doing: My six-inch bandaged thumb, flesh-beige and erect resting on my thigh right at the same angle of Nick's lumpy zippered lap next to mine, from T.J.'s hungover atilt as he squinted Popeye the Sailor Man to steady his depth perception to get a better look, looked like that of a six-inch penis. Nick's. Coitus interruptus in flagrante delicto. Like none T.J.'d ever seen before: uxoricidal casus belli (law school Latin was becoming dizzying). When Nick stood up to shake T.J.'s hand and the penis T.J. thought belonged to Nick remained attached to my wrist resting upon my thigh, T.J. saw it for what it really was: my busted throbbing thumb in a brace he hadn't seen because the orthopedic doc'd just strapped it on me yesterday.

"Glad to meet you at last, T.J. –" said Nick, assertively like the lawyer he'd never be. After some fumbling by T.J., used to the friendly slap on the palm giving five to his motley cronies he called his "bro's," the two men, as per quaint olde tradition, pumped *mano a mano*. "Ahhh—the famous missing T.J. At last. I've heard a lot about you."

"Oh, yeah?"

"You missed one hell of a party. A famous poet was here." Nick sneered when he said it.

"Oh shit! The party! Bukowski's party! I forgot all about it!" T.J. slapped his sunburned forehead to kickstart the conked-out memory bank inside. "How could I've forgotten? Shit!"

"Everyone waited for you, our groovy Godot, all night. Especially a woman named Big Mama."

"Oh yeah?" T.J. smiled, fondly remembering Lusty Linda, no doubt her derriere and the way she wore her hair when she cooed to him, "Oh, T.J., what big biceps you have" when she flicked an imaginary piece of lint off his tank top that read "Do It In the Road" that night after Bukowski read at the university and the four of us went out for drinks afterwards.

T.J. disappeared for two more days after he gave Nick a ride home to his worried wife. Like always, just hours before I was going to trek to the police department to file a missing person report, he showed up. Oh, that attractive nuisance, that other party I mentioned, the one that would change the course of my life. It happened June 6, 1975, right after I took my grueling two-hour Contracts I final exam, barely squeaking through it with a 1.75 (me gabbing erroneously on and on about disparagement and got even further off track with detrimental reliance instead of the correct cut-to-the-chase summary of per se breach of contract which I misspelled "breech"— how could 1?); 1.75 GPA the bottom line for any class in that law school, and I was feeling like shit anyway when I arrived home with my usual two bags of groceries plus toilet paper and dog food after my ordeal and saw the police helicopters circling my house. Then when I drove onto the street where I lived I saw at last the thousands of eyes peeking from the horizon of hell: hundreds of cars, motorcycles, dune buggies, pickups, RVs, bicycles, and skateboards parked all over the street and on my front lawn and driveway.

There must've been at least three hundred people (newspapers will cite five hundred), mostly teenagers, many bikers and hippies and thugs and firebugs and repulsive reprobates and debauched derelicts at Leah's Last-Day-of-School Party I'd told her she could have, could invite no more than twenty. That was the early days of copy machines in supermarkets and some funster had reproduced her invitation with a map and stapled it to telephone poles and hallway bulletin boards at three high schools.

The Party, The Fracas, The Melee, My Nemesis, whatever words to describe disaster, disillusion, and mayhem I could think of over the years to call it, would be not as much a free-for-all as it was a bad omen, a sign from wherever that I was *not* being admitted into the rarefied society of Lawyerdom that, in the length of time that it takes to call three hundred of your friends and tell them about a cute chick's beer bust (T.J. had bought four keggers), had become my LawyerDOOM.

That summer of 1975 turned out to be a hellish one for me, a true *saison d'enfer*, as I labored strenuously with my law studies, floundered in confusion, wondering whether I should keep on *carpe dieming*, or, truckin', as they called it in those days, or drop out of hell and go to the university and study what I really wanted to: French. Get a self-satisfying, miscreant master's degree in French, which would surely seal my fate as a failed careerist. My misery, though not half as bad as Linda King's and Charles Bukowski's who started fighting so bad and ugly they would soon break up for good in such a horrible way Linda would say: "Our love turned sick."

And I had nothing to do with it though Linda thought I did, and Bukowski said to me: "I believe Linda thinks that I am in love with you so you'd better not mention a casual friendship. Linda is ambitious, despondent, sex-oriented, and a damned women's libber. There is something about her energy that is fragmented and near-hysteria."

Her energy turned toward me, unfragmented, in the form of a steamroller, four-page, single-spaced typewritten letter wherein she accused me of being in love with Bukowski, setting up my Bukowski Bash just to get Bukowski off alone, have him all to myself. "Reach for the steel, sister!" she warned, prefacing each paragraph of her irate, kick-butt letter.

"What did I do to deserve this?" I asked Bukowski. "She thinks I want your body and if she ever hears about me having it she'll, and I quote: 'Beat the shit' out of me.'"

Bukowski laughed his har-har-har amongst the trumpets. He liked making Linda jealous. He liked it a lot.

"A hundred years from now, Bukowski, all these women of yours are going to make you seem like the biggest stud of this millennium replacing Lord Byron. You're responsible for all this, you know. I just want to be friends with Linda. And you. Why don't you two just get married, settle down in a nice little L.A. stucco home, make a baby, and write poems about Grecian urns? And I'll hang out with Rod McKuen instead."

"I am better than Rod McKuen. Besides, he's a faggot," Bukowski said. "Basically Linda's complexity is out for victory, that American-bred shit to win, win, win. Her basic lack of reality is that just to win don't win ya a cold hot dog. As the years grow shorter and the catch gets less close she becomes more vindictive, demanding, caustic, cantankerous…hell, you've got a dictionary. I'm drunk."

I begged Linda to believe me that I wasn't in love with Bukowski. I just wanted to be his friend. And hers, be a "sister."

"Don't give me that. You've become one of his groupies just like all these women hanging around wanting a piece of him. Disgusting. Friend, my foot."

"Linda, why would I want Bukowski when he's yours? I'm not a groupie, I'm your friend. I once was a go-go girl and knew the likes of Jim Morrison, Jimi Hendrix, Ike Turner, the Righteous Brothers, the Three Dog Night, met them at Whiskey's plus the Rivingtons and Chicago Blues guys and a lot of them quite tall and good looking and none of them was I ever a groupie for. Why would I want to be a groupie for a dirty old man like Charles Bukowski?"

"Because he's a genius. Because he's the most exciting man you'll ever know."

"It's true I want to fuck you –" said Bukowski one November night in 1975 when I was studying for Contracts II finals, calling me the week before he and Linda had their big, big fight and broke up for good, the melee he wrote about in his book *Women* except that that was his Black Sparrow story, himself as flustered hero, forlorn and embattled lover. Linda's version, the other way around. "—and it's true that I don't want to fuck you. Fuck ain't all that hot shit. I want flow. You don't matter that much to me and neither does Linda. I don't know what to do with her. If only she would get off her brutality-domination kick and simply breathe in and out. I mean, what the hell, how much bacon can you eat?"

After Linda left him for good, selling her house in Los Angeles and fleeing in fury to Phoenix, Arizona, where she stayed, Bukowski, drunk as usual at midnight, called me: "Linda, Linda? Is that you my beauteous woman? My woman with little green and golden moths sewed against the sides of her cunt? Love, Linda, is not having to pretend that you care. Remember, Linda?"

"This isn't Linda, Bukowski," I said. "It's Joan."

"Ohhh, it's you. Jo-o-o-an, Joan. Jo-o-o-an, you have a way of sounding like all women. Shit. All you women are either named Linda, Smith, or Joan." He hung up and called, I suppose, the real Linda.

On his fifty-sixth birthday, August 16, 1976, Bukowski called so I could wish him a happy birthday. I was quite depressed. It was the tenth anniversary of the day my second husband had tried to kill me with his bare hands. Feeling sorry for myself, I told him about the awful night that Othello defenestrated through my living room window, glass crashing all around— "Aww, yeah," he said, "August 16,1966. Remember it well, kid. A bad day for both of us."

Seven more years Charles Bukowski amused me at the standing-room-only readings I attended, a couple more midnight drunken phone calls, his fabulous letters until he finally married (not the First Linda), got rich off his poetry and a screenplay, and never spoke to me again. Linda and I stayed friends. In 2001, when the State of California's legal system has a seven-year backlog of impending litigation created by the largest glut of attorneys-at-law in the USA, and years after T.J. is a long-ago nightmare I had when I lived on Agony Way, and I am married to a poet and Bukowski dies of leukemia instead of by the blood-besotted hands of a beauteous jealous woman screaming from a balcony, when Linda calls one hot, full-moon June 2001 night, she will finally tell me that Bukowski told her how we'd been lovers. That sneaky bastard. That sneaky dead bastard. I will vehemently deny it.

"Don't lie to me," Linda will snap at me. "You were crazy about Bukowski."

True. I was crazy about Bukowski. But he also terrified me. I wasn't brave enough to be one of Bukowski's women. Not one of his real women, scream at him from a balcony, wrestle with him, love dog from hell, get down south of no north then flop wantonly onto a water bed to kiss and make up. One kiss from him was all I could handle.

That night of my Bukowski Bash, just as he was leaving, Linda in my garage getting her purse and car keys, Bukowski and I alone for the first and only time, standing in my doorway. Six inches-plus-two taller, crouching over me, Bukowski looked down on me. So drunk his out-of-focus eyes slit snoozing cat's, so mind-blotto'd he did not know who he was, did not remember that he might be one of the greatest American poets of them all, he took me in his arms and kissed me, his tongue a sponge mop in my mouth, so startling me, so terrifying me, I got sick. Maybe it was all the cheap champagne that caused my queasy stomach.

"Bukowski! Get your sorry ass out here! Else I'm leaving you to walk home to L.A.!" shouted Linda from the curb outside my house where her funny-looking vehicle was parked. Bukowski, jerking to sobriety as he must've remembered how egregious the thirty-five-mile walk from suburbia to L.A. alongside the freeways San Diego, Santa Ana, and Hollywood, let me go and staggered on out into the April dawn, the morning after the *Titanic* sunk sixty-one years before, three days before Lincoln died one hundred and ten years ago, stealing a kiss from me meaning absolutely nothing to him, merely something piddling he did every day like sipping coffee, petting his cat, kicking a beer can out of his garden, because he never, ever mentioned kissing me. For me, though, drenched and dizzy from it, the secret sin of it, I felt like his accomplice in the last Great Train Robbery, Pinkerton Men all around, me all alone left holding the bag.

"I was crazy, all right, but I was never crazy enough to be Charles Bukowski's lover," I will in June 2001 avow to "Lydia Kane" (as Buk called her in *Women*).

"Oh, how the lady doth protest too much," she will snidely sneer, my so-called "sister." "Sure you were. Those were the best years of your life. You were lovers with Bukowski, all right. You might as well admit it. He was a genius. He was absolutely amazing. He was the most exciting man you'll ever know. How could you possibly have resisted him?"

Linda King, my never-be sister, will always like her mister, her Charles Bukowski best.

(Street Art, Paris, France)

"There is that which helps you believe in something else besides death."

CHARLES BUKOWSKI
"One for the Shoeshine Man"

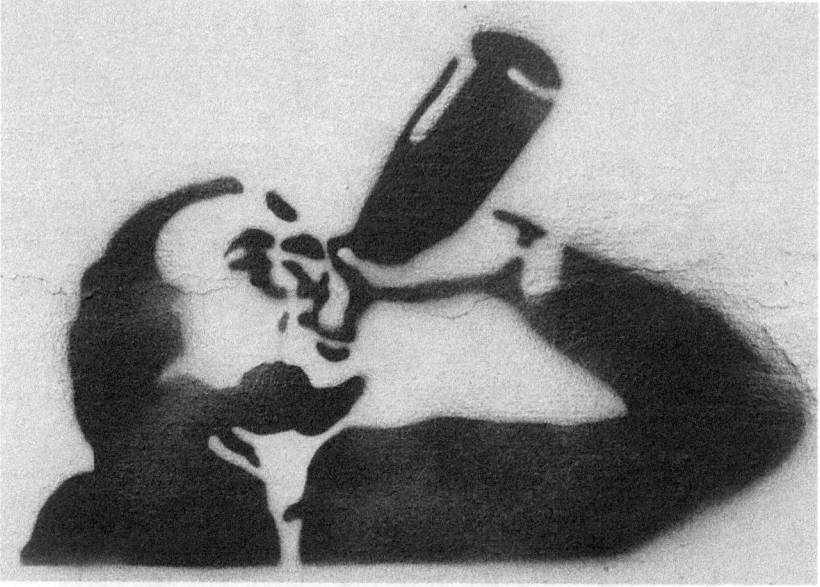

(Street Art, Germany)

"That's the problem with drinking, I thought, as I poured myself a drink. If something bad happens you drink in an attempt to forget; if something good happens you drink in order to celebrate; and if nothing happens you drink to make something happen."

CHARLES BUKOWSKI, *Women*

POST SCRIPT TO A BEER CAN IN THE GARDEN

ON GOOD FRIDAY, APRIL 6, 2012, NINE DAYS BEFORE THE hundredth anniversary of the sinking of the Titanic, thirty-seven years after the April 11, 1975 party I gave in Bukowski's Honor (and to celebrate *Pearl#3*), the First Linda, Linda King, aka Linda King, telephones from San Francisco after I'd left several messages on her Facebook page.

I hadn't heard from Linda King in months and wondered how negotiations were going on the sale of her Bukowski memoir, *Loving/Hating Charles Bukowski*. She'd emailed it to me for a blurb, two hundred plus pages devoted to, as dramatized by Linda King, the First Linda—the intensely ambivalent grand passion True Story A-B-Cs of Bukowski's audacities, bombastics, and complexities. Parts of her memoirs had been published in UK's *Beat Scene* and the Bukowski Symposium Newsletter in Germany. I'd heard she'd sold the entire book for publication.

"No, not yet," she says. "But my son's still trying to get investors up in Canada to make it into a movie."

What a movie it would make, I say. A *lot* of action, I say. Linda laughs.

"That's for sure. Bukowski and I saw a lot of action."

Yes, maybe as much as World War II, I say—or one thousand Super Bowls. Linda King laughs again—her easy and frequent laughter is one of the traits that makes her so lovable.

Five years before, I read online that she'd sold a large quantity of her letters from Bukowski for sixty-nine thousand dollars—netting just twenty thousand after taxes and fees. A single letter Bukowski wrote in the 1980s to Ann Menebroker had sold on eBay in 2009 for fifteen hundred dollars—the seller not Annie, but someone to whom she'd given the letter.

Linda King begins to tell me about the latest poetry readings in San Francisco and her sculpted heads on display at North Beach's

Beat Museum: Bukowski, Jack Micheline, A.D. Winans, Neeli Cherkovski, Robinson Jeffers, Ferlinghetti, Jack Hirschman and Harold Norse. I ask if she was ever going to sculpt Neal Cassady or Jack Kerouac.

"Been working on Kerouac. Shot some pictures of his head, side views, frontal, but can't find any of the back or the top of his head. I'm not really too inspired to do Jack Kerouac, anyway. I like to know the poet or writer personally, feel his soul and spirit. And Jack Kerouac was such a womanizer. I get angry at him when I read what he wrote about women. I can't sculpt a head when I don't like the person."

Bukowski was a womanizer, I say.

"Oh, not really. And back in 1972, I was young and I was falling in love with him when I sculpted his head so I liked him a lot!" She laughs.

While I talk to Linda on the telephone, I'm standing in front of a reproduction of that Bukowski head that sits on my roll-top desk. My husband, poet Fred Voss, bought the head from Linda King in 1996 for fifteen hundred dollars—a marvelous, life-sized bronze head, sculpted as he looked at age fifty-two.

Bukowski wears a big, happy grin and my husband's khaki broad-brimmed hat. At Christmastime, we put a Santa hat on Bukowski—making him appear magnanimous. And in my husband's grey and black beanie cap, Buk looks like a stevedore. But Bukowski seems strange wearing a baseball cap. And a fez. Especially a sombrero—and a burnoose doesn't suit him. Neither does a Greek fisherman's cap, a Fred Astaire top hat nor a derby. A beret makes him appear drunk. He looked delightful in a tall-top red-and-white-striped Cat in the Hat, but Fred made me take it off. "You're desecrating my Bukowski," Fred said. And Fred wouldn't let me put Mickey Mouse ears on Bukowski, either. Bukowski'd look handsome in a Busby, I'm sure. Or a pirate's hat. And I've wanted to try a turban on him—I'm sure he'd look magnificent as a swami.

"But I've been angry at Bukowski lately," Linda King goes on. "Started remembering that old porn piece about a child molester he wrote for *Hustler* magazine back in the 70s. We really had a big fight over that. I called him a pedophile and kicked him out of my house, made him move into his own place after that. He said he didn't really think like that, that he just wrote it for the money. But I don't think people can write things they don't really believe in, that they wouldn't do themselves."

The Intentional Fallacy, I remember from my literary criticism class in grad school. Wimsatt and Beardsley's 1954 *The Verbal Icon*. The intentional fallacy, according to them, "forces the literary critic to assume the role of cultural historian or psychologist who must define the growth of a particular artist's vision in terms of mental and physical state at the time of his creative act." Sigmund Freud and Carl Jung might've agreed with Linda King's theory of the source and depths of Bukowski's pornographic imagination. I felt the same as Linda King back in 1975 when I read the *Hustler* story. I bawled him out. Asked him what would his daughter Marina say or feel about it when she became a grown up and read such a thing written by her father.

"I'll tell Marina how I did it for the money," Charles Bukowski said.

Now today, I recall one of John Updike's rules for literary criticism: "Do not imagine yourself a caretaker of any tradition, enforcer of any party standards, a warrior in any ideological battle... Never, never try to put the author 'in his place'... Review the work, not the reputation."

Linda King dreams a lot about Charles Bukowski. I often dream of him, too. In my dreams, he's always insulting me, says I'm fat or old. Linda King also has recurring dreams of elephants and had one the other night of her and Bukowski riding on one.

Where were you guys going? I ask.

"I don't know."

Have you ever ridden on a real elephant?

"No."

You should, I say. It's unforgettable—all the terrific titanic strength and power an elephant possesses in its enormous bones. Maybe your dream represents your unforgettable journey through Khyber Passes of recovered subconscious emotion and your remembered time with Bukowski.

"Yeah, for sure, because when I woke up I remembered how he once blacked my eye." Linda King does not laugh—her voice is tinged with sorrow I've never heard from her before.

"Neeli Cherkovski told me I should stop thinking and saying bad things about Bukowski. Neeli says Bukowski wasn't really that bad of a man. But really, there weren't many good, happy times. Bukowski could be such a monster. Bukowski had brain damage, you know, from all his decades of hard drinking. A doctor told him back in the 1950s, after he was hospitalized for a long drinking binge with bleeding ulcers and almost died, that Bukowski'd die young if he didn't quit. Bukowski wrote a lot of poems about it. You know how obsessed Bukowski was about dying. He'd had an out-of-body experience. And after that drinking bout, alcohol affected him differently. It didn't take much to make him drunk and crazy. After three beers, he was on his way and you'd best get out of his way."

So, here it is Good Friday and we're crucifying Charles Bukowski, I say to Linda King, making her laugh again.

"Good Friday? I didn't know. Well, Bukowski was no Jesus Christ, that's for sure, though he took Christ's name in vain a lot."

And it's nine days away from the hundredth anniversary of the sinking of the Titanic, I say to Linda King. The night of my Bukowski party back in 1975, it was almost the sixty-third anniversary.

"He was really an ass that night," Linda King reminds me.

A beer can in the garden, he called himself that night, I remind Linda King. I almost tell her about the French publisher 13eNote recently translating an excerpt about Bukowski from my memoir "Une Canette de Biere Dans Le Jardin" as a post face in their reprint of Bukowski's *Shakespeare Never Did This*. But I don't. I've always preferred listening to Linda King tell what's happening to her. Linda King's always been more interesting to me than I am.

"Bukowski sure hated those law students and that one poet you invited to that party. That's one of the worst drunks of his, ever. He'd been drinking two days. He drank his own urine from a champagne bottle that night."

Did he *really*? I ask. I hated the thought he'd do something like that.

"Oh, who knows what he really did. But Bukowski said he did. So that's just as bad," Linda King concludes.

Illusion vs. Reality. Intentional Fallacy vs. Imagination. Charles Bukowski, eighteen years, four weeks, five hours dead on Good Friday 2012, still astounds Linda King and me with his ancient, unforgettable, perpetual paradoxes and officious intermeddlings with our memories and dreams. And I guess Charles Bukowski, lumbering, reliable, beer-soaked Love Elephant from Hell, always will.

> *"well, there's beer...rivers and seas of beer*
> *beer beer beer...the radio singing love songs*
> *as the phone remains silent... and beer is all there is."*

> — **Charles Bukowski**

CHARLES BUKOWSKI VEGETARIAN CHILI

At a party I held in Charles Bukowski's honor back in 1975, I served a version of this vegetarian chili along with a meat chili. Around dawn, Bukowski had drunk sufficient alcohol to get hungry, but the meat chili I'd made was gone, with only a bowlful of the vegetarian chili remaining. Bukowski was not inebriated enough to buy my claim that the cauliflower floret he'd spooned into his mouth was a chunk of chorizo sausage. Turned out, Bukowski was a fairly knowledgeable cook and a budding vegetable gourmand. Earlier, he'd scoffed at the festive magnums of champagne I'd bought for him, saying, as if he knew for a fact: "Even Cary Grant hates champagne." Bukowski, though, did savor the vegetarian chili—and the cauliflower floret, too...

AMOUNT	INGREDIENT
2 TBS	Extra virgin olive oil or lard
1 Cup	Yellow onion, chopped
1 Cup	Red/purple onion, chopped
3 TBS	Garlic, minced
2 Whole	Serrano peppers or jalapeño peppers, seeded/minced
1	Medium zucchini, diced
1/2 Cup	Carrots, diced
1 Cup	Fresh corn kernels (about 2 ears)
1-1/2 lbs	Crimini or button mushrooms, cubed
1 Cup	Fresh cauliflower florets (optional)
2 TBS	Fresh chili powder
2 TBS	Ground cumin
1 T	Ground coriander
3	Large fresh tomatoes, peeled, seeded, chopped
4 TBS	Tomato paste
1-1/4 tsp	Kosher or sea salt
1/4 Cup	Cayenne powder
1/4 Cup	Chopped Cilantro
2 Quarts	Joan's Own Almost-Texas Pinto Beans with broth

DIRECTIONS:

— In large pot, heat oil or lard on medium-high heat and sauté red and yellow onions until soft, about 2-3 minutes.

— Add serranos or jalapeños and garlic and sauté 30 seconds.

— Add zucchini, carrots, corn, mushrooms and cook, stirring until vegetables brown slightly, about 5 minutes.

— Add chili powder, cumin, coriander, salt, cayenne, cook and stir, until fragrant, about 30 seconds.

— Add fresh tomatoes; stir well.

— Add 4 tablespoons tomato paste and 2 quarts pre-cooked Joan's Own Pinto Beans with about 1 cup of bean broth (if canned beans are used, drain off liquid).

— If desired, add 1/2 cup favorite beer or 2 Tbs (or more) of good whisky.

— Stir, bring to simmer.

— Add more water or bean broth, if needed, to become the thickness of chili you desire.

— Reduce heat to medium-low and simmer, stirring occasionally, about 10 minutes, watching carefully. Beans can burn quickly and are ruined when scorched.

— Turn off heat. Let set 10 minutes, covered.

SERVING SUGGESTIONS:

Serve over brown rice.

Top with salsa, sour cream, or plain yogurt.

Garnish with cilantro leaves, diced avocado, or large washed Romaine lettuce leaves as "spears" or "spoons" tucked into sides of soup bowl.

Serve with corn bread, tortilla chips, quesadillas, crusty bread, saltines, or warm corn or flour tortillas.

Illustration by Henry Denander

"I was born to hustle roses down the avenues of the dead."

CHARLES BUKOWSKI

LOVE, BUKOWSKI

Commentary by Joan Jobe Smith

FEROCIOUSLY HOT, DRY, THE TYPICALLY INCLEMENT, extraordinarily maddening dystopia Charles Bukowski often described L.A. in his writings, raging wildfires engulfed mansions and manzanita in nearby Malibu hills on September 29, 2005, the day we went to see the play *Love, Bukowski.*

Black fingers of smoke deathscape strokes from a van Gogh lost painting streaked the sunset sky as choking smog blanketed the Los Angeles basin. Ash covered the downtown Long Beach main street freeway exit called Broadway and the sidewalk leading up to the repertory theatre ticket window, where a homeless man begging for coins complained how the theatre manager wouldn't let him use the restroom facilities. Then, noticing the bail bonds next door to the theatre—bright lights boasting, "Anytime, Any Jail"—I said out loud, a mindless mantra I've repeated since Bukowski's March 9, 1994 death: "Bukowski would've loved this."

Many Bukowski readers and his old friends tell me that they, too, often say of the dependably opinionated, been-there-wrote-that Bukowski: "Hank would've loved/hated this" whenever global disaster, war, good news, or comeuppance happens or they happen upon a quirky human interest piece in the news. Recently, someone wrote me, "Sure would like to read the poem Buk would've written" about California anti-cockfight activists' suggestion that roosters wear boxing gloves.

My last communication from Bukowski, then ailing, was in May 1992, in the wake of the second Los Angeles riots, "I've seen more cops surrounding me on a freeway when I was drunk. Like before

(1965 Los Angeles Watts riots), they suggested we pray. Anarchy is just a belch away. Ow, ow, ow –" Passionate expounder of first-person, provocateur of paradoxical hypocrisies, Bukowski never failed to impress devoted readers or put off put down critics with his world-weary poetic punditries cum proletarian vodka veracity.

Americans so angrily at odds with each other, dogmatically divisive these days, taking pro-con blue-red sides on every issue from politics, religion, what new celebrity dresses best, to Charles Bukowski, I wondered what stance artistic director Joanne Gordon would take regarding the controversial, love-him-or-hate-him poet/writer, and now emerging American cultural icon, Henry Charles Bukowski, Jr.

For the sake of sensational theatre, would she portray the raunchy antiestablishmentarian Henry Chinaski persona Bukowski parlayed by a nose on the inside rail in many of his down-and-dirty writings some critics called "coarse and vulgar"? Play up the romantic Love Dog from Hell of the 1995 BBC documentary? Or would she go for the audience's heart, and formalistic academia-and-corporate-run literary approval, and lionize Bukowski as misunderstood accessible-narrating dead saint of American literature by cleaning up his act, sewing his beer-soaked sow's ear silk etoi and emphasizing his skid row habitué rehab to rico americano screenwriter in epaulet-shouldered shirts lapping Liebfraumilch, noshing steamed veggies—as did producer-director John Dullaghan's 2004 *Born Into This*?

Since I'd heard Ms. Gordon had created and performed *Love, Bukowski* in 1990 with Bukowski's approval, I expected the latter. Until, upon entering the small repertory theatre, sold-out seating capacity about one hundred, I saw beyond the footlights of beer mugs and half-full Budweiser bottles, the main prop at center stage: a gleaming Cyclopian commode, optic nerve-scorching as an August dog day noon sun.

Unexpected, exciting, utterly alive and lovable as Bukowski was in person, *Love, Bukowski,* Ms. Gordon's intuitive and intelligent selection of some of the best and evocative of Bukowski's voluminous slice-of-life writings, well-performed by capable actors and actresses, young and aging, speaking from their hearts enabled by talented instinct and not presumptuous, interloping Bukowski emulation, the ninety-some minutes of *Love, Bukowski* showcases, above all, Bukowski's soulful humanity.

Within this satisfying and seamless sequence, Ms. Gordon has captured the heart of Bukowski in her hands, as well as his true grit, guts, unrelenting audacity, and instantaneous wit, sans coarseness and only an occasional vulgarity—the sight gag commode flushed only twice, only once for the contrivance bathroom humor, and as punctuation, at that. Other than Bukowski's legendary live poetry performances I witnessed in the 1970s, Ms. Gordon and her fine cast's depiction of the inimitable artist, poet, and man is the closest I've seen to the real Bukowski—and it took an ensemble to do it.

Lucky enough to have known Charles Bukowski personally 1974-1984, I was one of his peripheral editors and an occasional epistolary-long-distance telephone pal. Lonely, between women, Bukowski often called me after midnight, sometimes so drunk he called me Linda or Jane. The times he called sober just to talk, I made him laugh uproariously at my unabashed admiration of him and my gushing proclamations of his greatness. No actor less imposing than an Orson Welles could reproduce the laughter that came fast and easy for Bukowski and that was described best in words from one of his poems: "har-har amongst the trumpets."

Confident egoist, he'd brag to me about his latest literary success, sold-out reading tours for which he was asking (and getting) exorbitant fees, the completion of *Factotum, Women, Ham on Rye*. Genuine fan, I'd oblige him with: "Someday, Bukowski, they're going to name you the Greatest American Poet of them all."

"I already am the greatest American poet," Bukowski'd say, meaning it.

"Epic glottis," I pronounced him one night.

Har-har, he laughed. "I like your way with words, especially your words about me," he said, enjoying my fractured flattery.

"Someday you will win a Pulitzer, a Nobel –" I said, the summer when he was especially down, his long-time love, Linda King, gone for good.

"I'll be dead before then –" Bukowski said on his birthday, August 16, 1976.

We talked a lot about death that night, the coincidental tenth anniversary of a domestic tragedy in my life with an ex-husband I'd come to call Othello. Lugubrious, inebriated, and emboldened on wine, I told Bukowski what had happened that 1966 night. Seen-it-all Bukowski, his face as pocked as miles of bad road to prove it, could be told anything.

"Bad night for both of us," he said, unflappable. "Birthdays and attempted murder. Nothing worse than those."

Autodidact, innate scholar, as knowledgeable of literature as any Ph.D. professor I'd know in three years when I became a graduate student at a prestigious California university, Bukowski corrected me for likening myself to Ophelia.

Instead of commenting on my self-pitying melodrama, he said: "Better get your Shakespearean tragediennes straight, kid, or you're going to be the laughingstock of grad school. Desdemona was Othello's wife. And kid, you gotta remember the most important thing of all. You didn't die."

"Hey, Bukowski!" I heard a feminist holler from the front row of Bukowski's August 16, 1975 poetry reading at the Laguna Beach Moulton Theatre. Shag-haired, angry, chauvinist-pig-hating, wanting-it-all-now, feminists liked to pack the front rows at Bukowski readings wherever they were performed to heckle him relentlessly, then stage a walkout. "Why is it you write so much dirty poetry?"

"Give me an example of dirty poetry," Bukowski shot back, calmly, then, enraging the women more, guzzled vodka and orange juice from a pint bottle wrapped inside a brown paper bag to prove what a pig he was. No male writer in the western world of literature that I know of has been as profoundly hated by women (who said so) and as equally profoundly loved by women (who said so) as much as Charles Bukowski.

"Why don't you ever write poetry about your mother?" the feminist fired back.

"My mother died before I was born," answered Bukowski.

"Hey, Bukowski! When are *you* gonna die?"

"I die every day. We all do."

Joanne Gordon's Bukowski-still-lives production, had she eliminated the title's comma, might've been an imperative from Ms. Gordon: Love Bukowski—or else. Instead, she titled it, as Bukowski complimentarily closed many of his letters to friends, women and men alike, eponymously, "Love, Bukowski."

Setting the stage just right, allowing his fabulous, and often great, work to speak for itself, letting Bukowski introduce himself and tell his own stories through these varied Everyperson voices, the wise, ostensibly loving Joanne Gordon let her audience fall in love with Bukowski and his incredible Odyssey life, times, and wondrous women for themselves, reestablishing, reaffirming in 2005 what made Charles Bukowski so popular right off: his right-on, breathtaking truth, his boundless capacity for capturing loving hearts, and, most of all, Bukowski's own indefatigable ability and generosity to love back.

Joan Jobe Smith loving the *Love, Bukowski* poetry play, October 2005.

Bukowski would've loved this play as well as its close proximity to a brightly lit 24-7 bail bonds. Amongst the present buzz trumpeting Bukowski's possible greatness as a poet, amped up to high by his big press books doing good business, and the many rave reviews of *Love, Bukowski*, even in his hometown newspaper, the *Los Angeles Times*, usually dismissive of him and his work, perhaps the next locale for Ms. Gordon's production will be next door to the 24-7 bright lights on another Broadway, the real one.

Closing night, standing room only, October 15, 2005, another typically inclement Southern California day, a big storm coming tomorrow that will bring ferocious thunder, lightning, floods, blackouts, and mudslides to the L.A. hills and arroyos burned bare just weeks before, we waited outside the theatre on our Long Beach Broadway to meet up with three of Bukowski's most beloved muses: francEyE (Frances Dean Smith), his only child Marina, and his widow Linda Bukowski—Bukowski poems about them poignant standouts in the play.

Post-hurricanes Katrina and Rita, in the midst of our own worrisome L.A. storm warning, we wondered what Bukowski would say, if alive, about the devastation of his inspirational New Orleans where he lived mid-1960s when a drifter antihero (soon to settle down thanks to Marina's 1964 birth) writing poetry for Gypsy Lou and Jon Webb while they produced his magnificent *Crucifix in a Death Hand* (currently valued at five thousand dollars).

Then suddenly Marina appeared. I'd never met her before. Flashing a fast, easy smile, brushing wind-blown hair from her shining cheeks, she amazed me with her resemblance to her father, inheriting much of his spirit, all of his unflawed facial beauty, smoothed into femininity. Sure bet Bukowski would've loved that most of all.

From left: Joanne Gordon, producer, *Love, Bukowski*; Linda Bukowski (Charles Bukowski's wife), and Marina Bukowski (Charles Bukowski's daughter). Joanne Gordon went on to produce other Bukowski-inspired works for the stage. In November 2012, her theatrical collage *B.S.: Bukowski. Sondheim,* a musical theater piece that fused Charles Bukowski's poetry with the music and lyrics of Stephen Sondheim, opened to rave reviews at the California Repertory Company in Long Beach, where Gordon served as Artistic Director.

"my daughter is most glorious...her eyes are brilliant with the remainder of the day, and she's smiling."

CHARLES BUKOWSKI, "sitting in a sandwich joint"

From cover of *Bukowski Review* Number One

(drawing by David Hernandez)

"...I kneel in the nights before tigers that will not let me be... And I do not care."

CHARLES BUKOWSKI, "for Jane"

@ THE FIRST ANNUAL BUKOWSKI FESTIVAL, MARCH 28, 2009, WITH THE FIRST LINDA— LINDA KING

Article by Joan Jobe Smith

CHARLES BUKOWSKI WROTE ME IN 1976: "I LOVE WOMEN. MOSTLY when they love me" and on Saturday afternoon, March 28, 2009, we're on our way to Hollywood to attend the First Annual Bukowski Festival at the Elephant Theatre on Santa Monica Boulevard and see for the first time since 2001 one of the women who loved Charles Bukowski: Linda King, the First Linda, Charles Bukowski's best girlfriend and muse in the 1970s.

Not since the 2006 Bukowski induction into the Huntington Library, have we driven the Harbor Freeway through downtown Los Angeles sun-blasting, glare-bright sky-rises to the Hollywood-Pasadena Freeway interchange, a maddening traffic sprawl- -crawl that takes an hour to travel five miles.

Today, though, a rare L.A. day of clear blue sky makes us feel as glad as tourists escaping snowbound hometowns. The perfectly pleasant spring weather is so exhilarating, the usual eyeball-scorching reflections from the big city's zillion office windows now resembling diamond sparkle-bling, we forget about the nation's worst pollution hacking and hulking behind us from the Los Angeles Harbor and frivolously consider that ozone rhymes with ice cream cone.

"Sailing against a mountain backdrop," Bukowski once wrote, which might've described our car heading toward the Hollywood Hills. If Hank were still alive and kicking beer cans down the streets of L.A., maybe he'd be writing one of his I Love L.A. poems or drawing cartoon sunbursts, birds, and flowers on a love letter to a Jane, Frances, Annie, Cupcakes, or Linda.

Of all the women Bukowski wrote about and dedicated books to, I've enjoyed the amazement of knowing most of them, including Bukowski's widow, his Last Linda, Linda Lee Beighle—our last handshake happening at the 2006 Bukowski induction into the Huntington Library, where she received a standing ovation for her generosity in donating Bukowski's fabulous and valuable personal collection.

Off the Sunset Boulevard off-ramp, just past De Longpre Street, where Buk lived in the 1960s, and just blocks beyond Vine, a direct line as the crow might fly from the WOO of the Hollywood sign, if you could see the WOO for the million sky-poking palm trees, telephone poles, electric wires, and worn-out rooftops, Linda King waited for us as she camped out with her King cousin Marge in one of those L.A.-ubiquitous 1950s dingbat style motels.

Linda's come all the way from San Francisco for this First Annual Bukowski Festival at the Elephant Theatre on Santa Monica Boulevard, produced by her thirty-year-old son, Scott Dylyn Hall. Kit-and-kaboodle, just three weeks ago, Linda moved to Northern California from Phoenix, Arizona, where she'd lived thirty-some years. Linda's very tired but laughs "hello" anyway and hugs and pats us "how are you?"

The moving away was hard on her, leaving her Phoenix friends and sister Gerry King behind. Up north, though, she can hang with the famous San Francisco poets she's known for decades: Neeli Cherkovski, A.D. Winans, Ferlinghetti and his City Lights.

Phoenix, Arizona, is the desert town where Linda King fled, fed-up, in 1976 after she and Bukowski broke up for the last time in a knockdown, leave-town fury. Back then, Bukowski told me Linda had tried to run him over with her Volkswagen.

"Bukowski's a big liar," Linda says today, for the hundredth time. Yeah, she admits it's true she broke his typewriter when she threw it out the window.

"But that turned out just fine because John Martin [Buk's Black Sparrow publisher] bought him a new one, the expensive electric kind he'd been wanting."

We laugh at Bukowski's hellacious hypocrisy, her ha-ha funny past-tense depiction of it, and enable once again another scoundrel, even a Love Dog from Hell to become a lovable saint post mortem. Great to see Linda has not lost her infectious sense of humor throughout all the thick and thin she's survived.

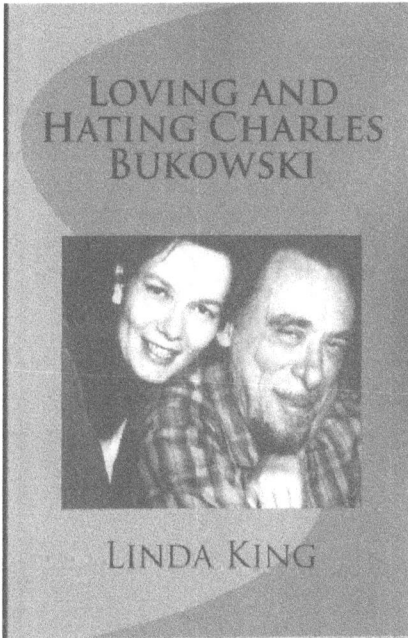

In 2012, Linda King published her memoir, *Loving and Hating Charles Bukowski.*

A cross between Mae West, Venus di Milo, and Annie Oakley, a wise-talking, straight-shooting diva-voluptuary, she's the type who can take up where she left off with you as if it were just a minute ago when it was really back in 2001. So we sprawl upon the sparse motel furniture, the punishing chair and squeaking beds and talk about everything from what ails us (the Economy, our tired aching backs, Linda's swollen hands) and then back to what regales us: Charles Bukowski—the why and how we all came to know each other in the first place. The cause celebre who caused our poetic effects.

"You shouldn't've ever moved away from L.A.," I say to Linda for the hundredth time.

After she left town, I missed like dinner her telephone calls of endless complaints about Bukowski. Often, we talked for hours about him and his heart crimes and crazy, drunken ways. Then nearly twenty years' worth of days ran away like wild horses over our hills, and we didn't speak again until 1994 when she was in L.A., where she was interviewed for a BBC documentary about Bukowski.

Linda sighs, says, wistfully, "Well, I wouldn't've moved away if Bukowski hadn't called the cops on me that night of our last big fight. They put me in jail. Hauled me away in handcuffs. That was very humiliating. Bukowski just went too damned far that time. Bukowski broke my heart."

So away she went to Phoenix, Arizona, unlocking herself from the arms of a crazy life. "Linda K. and I have rifted," Buk forlornly wrote me, "probably this time it's most permanent."

Outside the motel, after a quickie photo shoot against the backdrop of scrawny-dry Hollywood palm trees prettified springtime by a van Gogh aquamarine sky and pink-blossomed fruit trees, we take off for the Elephant Theatre a few miles away.

Ah, Santa Monica Boulevard! In the early 1980s, when I was still young enough to try to be cool, I knew this street well. Wearing fried crisp as tortilla chips permed hair and a baggy Virginia Woolf T-shirt and Hotlips camouflage pants, I hung out with writer friends in Silver Lake, karma chameleons, angst in their pants; went with them for falafel on Fairfax, Madame Wong's in Chinatown for heavy metal punk, saw Smokey Robinson at the Greek Theatre, Richard Pryor at the Palladium, Timothy Leary and Ginsberg at Al's Bar, first-run "Tootsie" at Grauman's, the first Gay Pride Parade.

Bukowski didn't live here anymore back then. "This is a great house," he wrote me in 1981 about his big home in San Pedro. "I bring my bottle up here to the second floor and type until 5 a.m."

Back then, before the film and television industry drifted away, traffic jammed Santa Monica Boulevard—today there's plenty of parking and the only moving vehicles on the street is a Harley and a boy riding a bicycle. Back then, the rich and famous and wannabes drove gold Cadillacs, Porsches, and junk-heaps down this street.

Down on that corner, in a 1930s-built cocktail bar, now For Lease, I saw Robert Mitchum sipping scotch, and, outside, Goldie Hawn and Buck Henry on the sidewalk waited for a green light. The glitzy Cinedome to the south, Rudolph Valentino's grave to the north, those Norma Desmond studio lots and shop spaces on this street grew old, unused and devolved, then evolved to the now-named Theatre Row. Ye Olde Hollywood drab stucco buildings spiffed up with mod-designer shades of burnt umber, black, verdigris paint jobs today ably house Hollywood's burgeoning art nouveau of energetic, ambitious, and hopeful young theater and independent filmmaking. Hollywood being Hollywood: Moving on. And on and on.

Inside the Elephant Theatre, everything's ominously black, brick and cozy—and I love it, feel as if I belong there, maybe should've been an actress, if I'd had talent. "Sex-sational!" I say to the interviewer, Kurt Brunghardt, director of the one-man show "Bohemian Cowboy," written by and starring Raymond King Shurtz that just finished a month's run to rave reviews.

"…three years ago, a cowboy walked into the desert and vanished…and the search continues…" Raymond's memoir began. That cowboy was Raymond's father. Raymond is Linda King's nephew, his mother Gerry King, Linda's oldest sister—inspired, indefatigable memoirists, those Kings. Gerry, now in her seventies, involved in theatre since her teens, has written many one-act plays and writes prolific entries daily on her blog. In 1975, I read her four-hundred-page novel, a love story, about Raymond's father.

"Fascinating," I told Gerry.

"Of course, it is!" she answered. Confidence—another inspired, indefatigable King family characteristic.

Sex-sational is an adjective I've always used to describe Linda King's hot-stuff vivacity. Kurt asks me questions about Linda and Bukowski's rocky relationship, which I count myself lucky to've only witnessed via telephone hearsay. "...if she would only get off her brutality-domination kick," Bukowski, 1975, wrote me his self-serving scenario—and then Linda would tell me *the truth*. Kurt plans to make a new Bukowski documentary, with Linda King as a substantial, significant plot line.

Charles Bukowski by Matt Sesow

After my interview, I see that the theatre has come alive with art by Matt Sesow, who's tacked fifty pieces of his vibrant, stunning hyperchromatic works on the black wall beneath the huge screen where we'll soon see Taylor Hackford's 1973 PBS documentary, *Bukowski*. Sitting on a table next to Linda King's racetrack paintings are two Bukowski heads Linda King sculpted in 1973—priced now at six thousand dollars each (foundry fee accounts for half of this figure). And soon the assorted Bukowski fans arrive: chimney-sweeps to slo-mo schmoozers and the young and restless nouveau cool Hollywood—Red carpet renegades decorated in posh-soft black leather, cashmere pashminas, designer jeans, and here-and-there Botox and rhinoplasty.

In 1975, when I was going to law school, taking a brief break from the literary world, Bukowski wrote me: "To hell with law. Feed your brain on me."

After the Taylor Hackford documentary, a big fat feast of Bukowski big-screen close-ups—Buk's face rocky as sixty miles of bad road—my parietal lobe is stuffed full of and possibly, fed up with the 1972 Charles Bukowski's extraordinary madness and ejaculation screams from a broken second-story window, and I feel bilious and ambivalent as I do when I eat chocolate cake for supper.

In 1972, at the kick-start zenith of his poetic fame and infamy for being a bad drunk, a cross between a godhead, a gin bottle, and a gorilla, Bukowski's last screen words har-har amongst the trumpets and treble in all our ears: "I don't think they can get to me now, man. The gold Cadillacs, the young blondes with the tight pussies, they came too late. The gods have really put a good shield over me, man. They've given me just enough, not too much. I've really got it. Christ, I've got it."

Ten years later, in his last letter to me before he married his Last Linda, a women-weary Bukowski wrote: "The novel *Women* was all right. All I had to do was to get drunk and sit down at the machine. The material was ready-made. I have long since stopped looking for the mate or even the ass…I figure if I kick off right now, I've already done ten times ten…"

Then begins the poetry reading by us *L.A. Poets who knew Bukowski*: Me, Gerald Locklin, and Linda King. *Those who almost knew Bukowski*: S.A. Griffin and Fred Voss. First Reader: Raymond King Shurtz, *the actor who, when a troubled teen boy, knew Bukowski*. From "The Great Drunken Poet" Raymond reads: "I'm standing in front of/the house on Edgewater Terrace/high on speed/yelling at the ghost of a poet/watching him vomit in the front yard ivy/…He lets out a howl when he sees me/"Where ya going', kid?"/"Up to my room, Hank, where you going, NASA?" Raymond King Shurtz's actor voice is manly, melodiously deep.

Number Two First Annual Bukowski Festival reader is Fred Voss, reading his panegyric published in *Das Is Alles, Charles Bukowski Recollected* (1994, Pearl Editions): "I had Bukowski/Somehow leading me out of the darkness & toward

Linda King and Gerald Locklin (2009).

the light/of finally finding my own voice & my own poetry/which I owe to him/as much as maybe my life."

S.A. Griffin, who didn't know Bukowski personally, also read from *Das Ist Alles* and talked about buying a Bukowski head from Linda King. A bronze one, S.A.'s Buk head sits on a table behind him next to the clay one Linda brought. These tandem, smiling side-by-side Bukowskis, these *twin happy Hank heads*, are an inestimably remarkable sight—magnificent memento moris, Cheshire Poet-Cat cheery postmortem comparisons to the barking beer-brawling Bukowski we've all just witnessed in the Hackford documentary.

Next Buk Poet, I was going to read from my novel, *Tales of An Ancient Go-Go Girl*, Chapter 13 about Bukowski, "Beer Can in the Garden" (*Beat Scene*, 2004) but the stage lights hurt my eyes so I improvise, tell the tale about the April 1975 night I gave a party in Bukowski's honor. Raymond King Shurtz, a troubled teen boy at the time, was there that night. Sitting in the front row this night at the Elephant Theatre, Raymond smiles and nods, remembering well my long-ago party. He was designated driver. Après party, on the way home from my house in the middle of the night, Bukowski pulled Raymond's hair, challenged him to a fight. Instead, infuriated Linda King had Raymond pull off the freeway, kicked Bukowski out of the car and made him walk the rest of the way home to L.A.

Next First Annual Bukowski Festival reader: the first academic to order Buk books from Black Sparrow for the CSULB bookstore and teach Bukowski's prose and poetry to his university literature students. Gerald Locklin surprises us Bukowski festival-goers by foregoing hagiography and literally doing a song and dance—a whimsical Shuffle Off to Buffalo tap dance routine and an impersonation of Johnny Ray's 1951 pop song "Cry."

Last First Annual Bukowski Festival reader is Linda King, the legendary First Linda, who reads from "Bukowski Undigested" (Purring Press, 2008, sesow.com) a recollection of 1970s love poems she wrote to Bukowski that includes new Bukowski-inspired poems, along with prodigious artwork by Matt Sesow, artiste extraordinaire and publisher. First time I've heard Linda King read since 1975, when I was her groupie, saw her read twice at California State University Long Beach and various bars. Back then, she always wore a sex-sational mini skirt or tight jeans.

In 2009, wearing red pants and jacket, her curly bangs forming a gentle shade over her bright eyes, her wizened voice still marked with a witty Utah-born twang, Bohemian cowgirl Linda King reads her falling-in-love-w/-Bukowski poems and poems about her ferocious kiss-&-make-up/break-up fights with Bukowski (Linda always having the last word and laugh).

Never hyperbolic bit instead narrative true stories, Linda reads her sex-sational poems: "A Cock" ("What is it?/It goes up, it goes down"), "Slug Lug," "Wrong Number," and "The Great Poet," where she makes us laugh with her metaphor of Bukowski as an orangutan, lumbering from her bed, eating oranges, "skinny arms/hanging from the elbows/belly bulging…announces he's going to take a crap/The only ape in town who/ Uses yards and yards of/Pink flowered toilet paper."

Linda King reads the poems about the end of their Great Love: "When These Days Are Over" ("I will remember/the beautiful curve of your mouth"), "Lovers" ("Unlocked as time/Continuing to some kind of/Undetermined eternity.") and last: "The Scar Still Shows":

> *He etched his name on my heart*
> *And though years have passed*
> *The scar of that name still shows*
>
> *As I read old words of love*
> *Tears flow from a well*
> *That should have long been dry*
>
> *In painful memory I return*
> *For a brief time and relive that time*
> *When our joy sailed forth as sunshine.*

@The First Annual Bukowski Festival, Hollywood, California, March 2009 @The Elephant Theatre (from left): S.A. Griffin, Joan Jobe Smith, Raymond Shurtz, Fred Voss, Bukowski head, Linda King, Gerald Locklin, and Scott Dylyn Hall (Linda King's son).

Ah, Linda, Linda. Linda King, you've captured our hearts in your hands once again with your extraordinary love for Charles Bukowski. And for the hundredth time made me so glad and grateful I never loved him. Oh, yes, I've admitted, all right, that I love him, but not *that* way, not Linda's way of loving: devoted diva, artiste of passionate conduct. I loved Charles Bukowski the way you love the moon, a white tiger, and your first bicycle—as objects of inspiration, admiration, and joie de vivre. Fun. What a man. What a Crazy Life.

Whether a poet pariah or essential avatar, what other poet on earth is as entertaining as Charles Bukowski? In his last letter to me ten years before his leukemia, his epistolary Adios after his do-it-himself ascension to his San Pedro hilltop house, in the midst of Barbet Schroeder's four-hour interview of him and the writing of his screenplay *Barfly*, Charles Bukowski wrote: "Take it easy, Joan. Life's bad, but not too much so."

And so, standing ovation at the Elephant Theatre, we Bukowski fans applaud Linda King and her amazing one-woman poetry show. We say goodbye to each other and the First Annual Bukowski Festival and its producer Scott Dylyn Hall (who will email me next week: "I'll make it better next year").

We exit the building and get home to Long Beach in only thirty-five minutes where I'll begin again to try to take it easy, wait for Linda King to telephone again, tell me what she's been up to, wait for a mockingbird to wish us luck while time burns the two of us in water while drowning us in its flame, our lives with and without each other and Charles Bukowski moving on. And on and on…

CHARLES BUKOWSKI'S GROUPIE
Poem by Fred Voss

After Frank and Jane have driven over the green Vincent Thomas Bridge from Long Beach

to San Pedro to go to Amalfitano's Bakery for Frank's favorite chocolate/walnut fudgies

Jane

tells Frank to drive by Charles Bukowski's house

driving down the hill with the port of L.A./Long Beach red cranes in sight Frank knows

the way by heart

"Look the trees have been pruned and you can see

the window of the room where Bukowski wrote!"

Jane says with delight

Jane has told Frank many times that Frank and Charles Bukowski are her favorite poets

and Frank looks for a few moments at the window where Charles Bukowski looked out

at the green bridge and the port's red cranes

and wrote

then Frank heads on down the street

"Let's go round the block and look at it again! I want to feel Bukowki's spirit!" Jane says

Frank lowers his brow and frowns

"Why would I want to see it again?" he says

"Why would I want to be Charles Bukowski's groupie?!"

Frank steps down harder on the accelerator

Jane once knew Charles Bukowski

in one of his letters he asked her to come do a Greek dance with him in his new house

on the hill

just because Charles Bukowski has sold thousands of times more copies of his books

than Frank has

and had several major motion pictures made of his work

doesn't mean Frank should drive around the block to look at his window again

Frank has his own window

where he writes and looks out at the next door apartment building's laundry room

and a red ACE HARDWARE trash can

and someday after he's dead he will be famous and people will cruise down 2nd Street

    in Long Beach

and point it out

after the gardeners have pruned back the fig tree in front of it

but as Jane says, "C'mon Frank!"

at the last moment Frank hits the brakes and jerks his arm and turns

his Toyota right at the intersection and starts the drive around the block like he has

dozens of times before

Why be small?

He'll never be able to drive by his own window

after he's dead

and a magnificent view of the 40-ton cranes in the largest port in the U.S.

sure does beat an ACE HARDWARE

trashcan.

Illustration by Henry Denander

"The world has changed me and I have changed what I can."
CHARLES BUKOWSKI

INTRODUCTION TO INTERVIEWS WITH LINDA KING, ANN MENEBROKER & FRANCEYE

by Fred Voss

(BUKOWSKI REVIEW, NO. 1, WINTER 2001-2002)

WOMEN: HOLDING THEIR OWN

PERHAPS THE MAJOR INSPIRATION FOR THE WRITINGS OF CHARLES Bukowski was women. Though accused in his own day by feminists of being a male chauvinist pig, a thorough reading of his work shows Bukowski to have deeply admired and even adored women rather than despised them—women that he lived with, drank with, laughed with, loved and fought with, strong women, wild, fiery women, witty women who could more than hold their own with him, who could get the better of him and leave him the comical butt of his own ridicule.

Having met three of these women in person over the years, I could see that they were indeed strong, intelligent, fascinating women, none of them a woman who could submit to the tyranny of a chauvinist pig. They were women of strong conviction, character and will and each had unique, special qualities that must have endeared her to a Bukowski who could not be bothered with run-of-the-mill beings but admired the different, the ones brave enough to find their own drummers to march—or dance—to. All were poets. All had their own poetic voice and were not about to silence it to suit Buk. Nor do I think Buk would have wanted silenced.

So, here are the interviews, one with each of these three women I had the good luck to meet who must have done much to inspire Buk to write some of his best lines and stories. They are all different, had different places in Bukowski's long and varied life, yet they all share the fiery power of a woman at her beautiful most enchanting best that Bukowski captured so well in his words. I hope you enjoy getting to know them as much as I did...

Linda King and Charles Bukowski fell in love during the months
she spent sculpting his head (above), which she completed
in 1972.

LINDA KING

Interview by Fred Voss

FRED VOSS MET LINDA KING IN DECEMBER, 1994 WHEN SHE was flown by BBC television to Los Angeles to take part in the filming of a Charles Bukowski documentary. This interview was conducted as they sat in Voss's living room in Long Beach, California, February 10, 2001, a sunny Saturday. Linda King had come to Southern California from Phoenix, Arizona, where she lived, to autograph one hundred broadsides, "Me And Bukowski."

FV: Linda, how long have you been writing?

LK: After I left college and came to California in the early 1960s. I had already written most of a novel, *Mad Oui-ja*, about my breakdown, by the time I met Bukowski.

FV: Linda, did you write as a child?

LK: Oh…no. My sister Gerry was a writer and got all of her sisters involved in writing. She was very adamant that we were all going to be writers, not just her. (Laughs.) So we all wrote…huge awful long letters. Ten-, twenty-page letters that developed later on into this little rag called *Half 'n' Half* of poetry, essays, stories, interviews and cartoons. It was quite an interesting little rag that only went between family and friends. And then in the early 1970s, we did five issues of *Purr* that was quite good. We had everyone in it: Steve Richmond, Gerald Locklin, Bukowski, etc…I ought to put out a book called *The Best of Purr. Purr* originally was supposed to be erotic poetry. Some of it was (laughs), but there was a lot of stuff that wasn't erotic that we ended up accepting. People did send me a lot of good stuff. I really enjoyed it. Gerry kind of killed *Purr* because she didn't like the poetry. She felt like she was giving her stories to little poems when they deserved a novel. (Fred laughs.) The Germans ask me about my regrets since Bukowski got so rich. I said if I had to give up what I had and take what Linda Bukowski

[Linda Lee Beighle, who Bukowski married in 1985] has, I would still take what I had. I got a lot of love, the physical love. He was older when he was with her. For all I know they had great physical love, too.

FV: You had some creative years.

LK: I had the best. Of course! I had the best! (Laughs.) The best! I was a liberated woman. I was determined not to take Bukowski's shit. If I had stayed with him I would have had to take a lot of shit, which I wasn't willing to take. He used to say that he hadn't had his women in his teenage years when he should have had them.

LK: Yeah, Bukowski used to write that in his poems how he had to make up for those years when he was alone and lonely. What "Germans" were you talking about?

LK: Falko Henning—he runs the Bukowski Society in Berlin. They gave me a hundred dollars to copy my sculpture (a head of Bukowski Linda King sculpted in 1972) for a plaque for the front of the building. I sold him Bukowski's sculpture for which he still owes me half (sips tea). It's hard to find someone you can really relate to and be in love with. That was the tragedy of Bukowski's and my relationship; it went to fame and fortune and the love got lost. I told Sounes (Howard Sounes, author of the Bukowski biography *Locked in the Arms of a Crazy Life*), that's why men get famous so they can have lots of women. For most men, that's what fame is.

FV: Do you think Bukowski in the early days expected that kind of thing? Fame, per se?

LK: Oh, I think he halfway thought he was going to be famous. He had his doubts and worries about it, but it was his plan.

FV: What Bukowski achieved as a poet has never been done before.

LK: No it hasn't…but…

FV: Edna St. Vincent Millay and Dylan Thomas were twentieth century poetry celebrities. Thomas did a reading tour of the U.S. and was a sensation. But then he died. Do you think Bukowski had him in mind? His extraordinary poetry fame?

LK: He used to talk about how they killed Dylan Thomas with the alcohol, but they weren't going to kill *him* (Bukowski).

FV: Yeah, he used to mention Thomas. Dylan drank fifteen straight shots.

LK: I don't remember Bukowski admiring Dylan Thomas's poetry. I think he thought it was too worked over. He worked and worked…

FV: Who did Bukowski like? Jeffers?

LK: He liked the easy straight line, not the complexity of line.

FV: Like Walt Whitman?

LK: Well…I think he liked Whitman, but….

FV: I can see Whitman in his writing.

LK: He loved Bukowski. (Laughs) That was the best. He always felt like his work was great. He would write at night, when he was drinking. He would clean it up in the morning when he was more sober. The clean up and straightening of the lines happened in the morning. You have to admit…think of it…just the amount of stuff he wrote. He wrote so much over the years. Anyone that wrote that much deserved to make it. There was hardly a night went by he didn't write.

FV: He worked hard. Truly inspired. Where do you think all of that creativity came from?

LK: He was a very smart guy. He was very smart. He had an energy. When you were around him in a room he could make the room live. If he got bored, he was apt to attack anyone who was boring him. He'd start insulting people. He wouldn't sit around and be bored like most people and think how are we going to escape. He'd either get rid of them or liven up the conversation. But sometimes he would get on these sulks. If I was having a party, he would sit out there and not talk at all.

FV: Bukowski was very much the classical music lover. How did you like that? Did you endure the classical music or enjoy it?

LK: I loved dance music, but he wasn't usually with me. I love classical music too. He hadn't learned to dance when he was young. He started dancing on his own after I took him to this party in Utah. I took him to a party where everyone was creating new dances. He didn't dance that night, but he learned something that night he used later. He used to actually dance at these parties. He would get up and dance like crazy. He added that to the Bukowski Show. You're just going to have read my book, *Charles Bukowski, In Passion and Fury* (Linda King's memoirs) if anyone publishes it.

FV: More secrets to come!

LK: Maybe I should serialize my book.

FV: I've read reviews where critics said they thought a lot of Bukowski's persona was fake, that he created a character in his fiction that was tougher or more streetwise than he really was. They suggest it was somewhat phony or made up. You knew him well. What's your opinion?

LK: Well, I think he probably did make up some of it based on what he wanted to be and to make a good story. But I think part of what he did, he had a very sensitive nature and he more or less wanted to cover his sensitivities. He didn't want people to think of him that way so he more or less put on an act. It wasn't a complete act and as he got drunk his personality went from his sober self to his drunken self so it was quite diverse. In the back of his mind, he had this image of what he wanted Bukowski to be so when he went out in public he played that image. He had to play it, and then became the drunken poet. He would act quite different at home.

FV: I've heard that after he became famous, he changed too.

LK; He wasn't too famous when I was with him. He always had this super ego. When I cut his hair once he signed the envelope [containing] his hair: "From the locks of the God, Charles Bukowski." (Laughs.) Partly he was being funny, but he was playing the role. He played this Bukowski thing to the hilt sometimes.

FV: Do you like his early poetry best?

LK: Not necessarily. He was trying to be more sophisticated in his first books. He later got more into the poetry for the common man. I fell in love with his writing when I first read it, the honesty of it. He would just come out and just be very honest about everything. A lot of the early poets are very veiled.

FV: Did you read him before you met him?

LK: I had asked around and Peter at The Bridge told me about him. That was the poetry hole in Hollywood where Bukowski did his first readings. It had a little bookstore in the front, but the back of it was just vacant walls and ragged furniture from the streets.

FV: In your life before you met Bukowski, did you have experiences that made you relate to his writing about being down and out?

LK: I had been writing. I was half way through a novel about my breakdown (in the early 1960s). But I had never lived down and out myself. I had married young and was taken care of by my Italian husband, divorced about a year before. My father had died and left me enough money to pursue my dreams of being an actress, artist, and a writer. When I got divorced, I started going to the poetry readings, jazz dens, etc. I had been to The Bridge numerous times. I remember Deena Metzger talking there after being fired from

UCLA. I had been going with a man I met there, Sylvan Paster-nak who was working with Cesar Chavez and the left-wingers. He was a very interesting man. I did a sculpture of him [Paster-nak] before [I did] Bukowski. He actually paid me for it. My writer sister, Gerry, suggested that I sculpt Bukowski so that we could meet him. I had been to his place with Peter and read him a poem that night, and they made fun of my poetry. I was afraid of him, and he was a drunk and he was ugly. Yet, I was quite taken with his writing.

FV: So at first you were not attracted to him?

LK: Not at all. I thought my sister Gerry might like him. I didn't start the sculpture for about a month. He no longer looked like the pictures I'd taken. He'd just lost his job [at the post office] and was drinking full time. He claimed he'd quit his job, but Sounes found out he'd been fired.

FV: What is your favorite Bukowski poem?

LK: I love the ones he wrote about me...of course. But my favorite poem not about me is "Have You Ever Kissed a Panther?"

FV: Joan [Jobe Smith] published one he wrote you in 1975, "the big ride" where he writes of "little green and golden moths sewn inside the sides of" your [bleep]... And I like that poem "Green Jell-O" that you wrote about the two of you making love in a bathtub filled with green Jello-O. [Fred and Linda laugh.] Linda, what have you been doing lately?

LK: I have an agent in New York who is trying to sell my book, *Charles Bukowski, In Passion and Fury*. Supposedly, it is going to be sold to a publisher. I was very excited just to get an agent in New York. It's very hard to do. Also, I have this broadside just out from *Free Thought* called "Me And Bukowski."

FV: Why don't you read the poem inside?

LK: Okay. "This Day Is Shot." This day has had it/This day has gone sour/And I'm doing to fuck it up more/I am going out dancing/and leaping and swaying and flirting/And you are going to be/so tired from the track/That you are going to bed/But I love to dance/And you love the track/I will dance...you will bet/I won't object to your sport/You won't object to mine/I'll see you/When I get back in the morning/Hopefully before you leave for the track/I'm sorry I couldn't wait for you/To come home from the horses/Like a good woman/And have a hot dinner waiting/But we are not married and a good wife/I am not/I may be a good fuck/But I might even lack that ability/I realized the last few months/Have been dominated by your desires/And I'm getting meaner by the day/Because I have given up/All the things I like to do/In favor of what you like to do/These feet like to dance/And dance they will/Dance...Dance...Dance/You said I would give you a hard time/Couldn't help it/You are right/I can't help it/It is good not to be married/So that I might please my self/I have a ten-year-long habit/Of trying to do what the man likes/But it is useless/Naturally you will assume this is a break/ you will run out to get as drunk as possible/But that is just another/Form of your blackmail/To keep me in line/You bad boy/If you get thirsty...drink/I can't worry if it kills you/It will kill you sooner or later anyway/If you die because I go dancing/It will only mean/Dancing has won/Drink like the wind/Drink like the stream/Drink, I demand you drink/Get deliciously drunk/So that your mind blacks out/And your soul flees/Drink, my darling/You can find many nurses/Drink like you were a god/And write how you sat with your/Bottle of beer/It is such a dramatic picture/The horses, the beer and the bad woman/This is all a great poet needs/I am the bad woman/And I have gone out to be bad/So that you can write more powerfully still/I do this to you."

FV: That's a beautiful picture of you and Bukowski (on the cover of the "Me & Bukowski" broadside). When did Michael Montfort take it?

LK: Around 1973, at Bukowski's place on Edgewater Terrace, I wrote this poem one day when he was at the track. I'll sign one for you. Now if we want to see Bukowski, in spirit, that's where we should go. I refuse to see his grave. I don't really believe there is a grave.

FV: My wife Joan used to go see you and Bukowski read all the time in the early 1970s. She said you and he had this call and response and would make some great jokes together.
LK: Bukowski always had a hard time being a couple in public. He had to be just Charles Bukowski. It seemed when we went out in public there was kind of a jealousy. He was always getting mad at me. Sometimes I felt like it was only a scene. He created a scene for the public. "You want to fuck her, etc.," and he'd threaten to fight some guy. That put pressure on me. It was kind of his Bukowski image and he played it to the hilt. I had him act in my play *Only a Tenant* and he was a great actor. He was adding lines, ad-libbing, etc. They should have put him in front of the camera in *Barfly* [the movie]. My play was about my living with him based on the premise that I could throw him out at any time. *He was only a tenant*, 1973-74. They made a cheapo movie in Malibu based on that play. The guy I was working with trashed my script. I left town and never saw the film.

FV: I looked at your book [a photograph album of all of King's sculptures]. A lot of the faces are very interesting. Tell us about them?

LK: Many of those heads are commissions. When I left Bukowski [in 1976], I opened a bar in North Phoenix [Arizona] I called "Linda's," and I was doing sculpture right in the bar. I had a couple of sculptures going at all times. I also painted about twenty or thirty pictures of the customers—cowboys, construction workers, roofers—that hung above the bar. I was getting two hundred dollars for a sculptured head. Thus the jokes: "She does two-hundred-dollar head jobs." One [a sculpted head] usually takes four sittings. I take pictures and work in between sittings from the pictures. Besides Bukowski, I did Jeffers from pictures. Lawrence Ferlinghetti, Jack Micheline, Harold Norse, Al Winans. I started Gerald Locklin, but he never came back to sit. I turned that one into the "Sea God." I would like to do a real one of him. I am supposed to do Neeli [Cherkovski] soon.

FV: What about the sculpture that Bukowski did? [Looking at a laughable, unphotographable blob of bronze that resembles a chunk of coprolite.]

LK: It looks like one of the little guys he used to draw. It is sitting with a hard cock. I named it "Chinaski." Bukowski never named it or signed it. I don't know what to do with it. I was offered two thousand dollars to reproduce it, but I can't because of copyright laws. It only took him about three minutes to make it. He was drunk and said, "I can sculpture better than you." He made three. He woke up and smashed all of them in the morning, but I saved this one and I have quite treasured it ever since.

FV: What's next, Linda?

LK: I'm hoping that my book about my years with Charles Bukowski will be a best seller and then my love letters [to Bukowski] will come out and they will be a best seller and I will become very famous and very very r-r-r-rich. I will travel worldwide. Europe. Read poetry.

FV: Do you think Bukowski was a male chauvinist pig or was he a great romantic?

LK: He was both. [Laughs.] He was a male chauvinist pig half of the time, and he was a romantic the other half of the time. He wrote some very romantic poems. Oh yes, and those beautiful love letters…and he could be a real shit.

FV: If Charles Bukowski appeared at the door right now, what would you say to him?

LK: Well, I don't know. I haven't been around him for a few years. We might be kind of strangerish for a while. It would be awhile before we got warmed up.

FV: Once you got warmed up, would there be something you'd like to tell him that you never told him?

LK: It wouldn't be just one thing. It would be numerous things. We'd be humorously testing each other. We had this chemistry between us and that wasn't verbal. I can't think of the verbal things. We'd probably want to head for the bedroom or something like that. He was actually quite shy. I imagine if he saw me after all these years, he would be quite shy. I would be too. He covered his shyness by being verbose. Since I left Bukowski, I have never been with a writer. Him and I related to each other in that realm. Most of the men I have been with are anything but writers. When I went to San Francisco and met writers again I thought, *"God, this is what I miss, somebody who can talk back."* Of course, Bukowski was also an artist. He did a lot of artwork that went into his books. He understood that side of my nature as well. He could give you your space to create. A lot of men can't do that.

UPDATE: In 2007, Linda King sold sixty of her Bukowski letters for $69,000 via PBA Galleries, netting $20,000 post-taxes and fees In 2012, King published, via Kisskill Press, her Buk book *Loving/Hating Bukowski* and Sore Dove Press published her memoir *Mad Ouija*. Linda King has reprised her "Head Job" sculpting enterprise, now charging five thousand dollars for two four-hour sitting sessions that include her regaling the subject with tales of Bukowski.

THE GREAT POET
By *Linda King* (1974)

he lumbers from the bed like a
three-hundred-pound orangutan
he can't find his glasses
he can't find his shorts
he can't find his stockings
skinny arms
skin hanging at the elbows
belly bulging
he throws sheets and quilts
in the air bellowing
farts noisily
scratches his ass with pleasure
he can't find his wallet
he can't find his shoes
hair and beard unkempt
he eats apples and oranges
by the dozen
makes strange noises to himself
expects others to understand
his hand signs and grunts
belches loudly in restaurants
announces he's going to *take a crap*
the only ape in town who
uses yards and yards of
pink flowered toilet paper

"Some people never go crazy.

What truly horrible lives they must lead."

CHARLES BUKOWSKI

Illustration by Henry Denander

From left: A.D. Winans, Ann Menebroker, and legendary outlaw
poet Kell Robertson at Vesuvio's, San Francisco, California (1999).

ANN MENEBROKER

Interview by Fred Voss

Ann Menebroker and Joan Jobe Smith first "met" in 1974 when Charles Bukowski urged Smith to solicit Menebroker's poetry for her first issue of *Pearl* when the magazine was funded by the Honors Program at California State University of Long Beach, and Smith was an undergraduate there. Ann and Joan's prolific epistolary-poetry friendship endured for more than a quarter of a century, with letters between them probably numbering in the thousands. Bukowski had met Menebroker in the early 1960s when he was an emerging poet on the American small press literary scene and dedicated *South of No North* to her. The following interview was conducted via mail, September 10, 2000, with Ann Menebroker writing from her home in Sacramento, California.

FV: Annie, what have you been up to lately?

AM: What I've been up to is what you've been up to, Fred, and this is: surviving. I just ended a ten-year job in an art gallery. In my attempt to find work that isn't absolutely mundane and prosaic, I recently started a new career in special education, where I am an instructional aide for middle school children. I like the kids, and I'm working on a collection of *Selected Poems* to be published by Red Cedar Press, Colorado, in 2001.

FV: What event in your life or the world has most astounded you?

AM: There are just too damned many prime experiences I've had in my life to make a single choice. I've been reduced to tears at music concerts, been to some outstanding poetry readings, the first landing of a man on the moon was pretty incredible, but I didn't go. I've seen sunsets and sunrises and the ocean and mountains and all of those drop-dead scenes in nature, been with men and/or family/friends in special moments; sometimes I've seen a member of my family in a perfect non-pose, with natural backlighting and it takes my breath away. But if anything has astounded me to the point of complexity, it is that none of us ever seems to remember how insanely wonderful being alive is! We break it all down into cultural differences and races and religions and politics and friends and enemies and geographic borders and economics and on and on, ad nauseam. Sitting home with a glass of wine and some good music, either alone or with someone I like, is astounding!

FV: It's my understanding that you first began to write poetry during your first marriage, in your late teens. Who/what were your first Muses?

AM: I began writing poetry at fifteen years of age. I began to take it a little seriously by the age of ninetten. I was turned on by romance, love, the ocean, fear, teenage despair, and being misunderstood. Those were my muses.

FV: Which poets have amazed or influenced you?

AM: Thomas Merton, Walt Whitman, Edna St. Vincent Millay, e.e. cummings, Gwendolyn Brooks, Anne Sexton, Sylvia Plath, Charles Bukowski, and many, many more. These are just the names I started with that stirred the fire. That heated me up. But I don't want to sit down and write a list of names of poets I have loved and respected over the years. They would be fine and worthy names. And the list would be very long. They would be an anthology of people I care about! Most of them are still around, and I am in touch with them. They know who they are.

You met Charles Bukowski in the early 1960s when he'd just been "discovered" by *The Outsider* magazine and the two of you were just starting out as serious poets. How did Bukowski affect your writing? Your life?

AM: I'd been getting some things published starting in 1957. But I was publishing under a different name: Ann R. Bauman. That's who I was when Bukowski and I began our correspondence. That's the name he wrote in his books and mailed to me: *Crucifix in* *a Death Hand, It Catches Its Heart in My Hand* —Works of Bukowski's beautifully published by Lujon Press in New Orleans. Bukowski was writing to me from there when he went to help these good people with his books. He and I were being published in some of the same mags. He had already begun to make a name among the poets and editors with his work. He was different—the way things are when someone is touched with uncommon talent and separated from the crowd. Combining his letters with the poetry I saw in the little's [small literary magazines], I thought he was one of the most fascinating poets on the scene. And we added phone calls to that. I was moved through my admiration of the strength of his work to become what I hoped was more authentic in my poetry. In the end, we write the way we can write and think the way we want to think and no crowd or single person is going to make a hell of a lot of difference. But what he did was release the "bug up my ass." He made me feel like a wilder sort of person. The actor from the 1950s, Sterling Hayden, once wrote: "In the worship of security we fling ourselves beneath the wheels of routine—and before we know it our lives are gone." Bukowski, I believe, was terrified of this kind of living—The Suburbia of the Heart. Something in his earlier years made him angry at daily living, jobs, survival, buying a new couch, celebrating holidays, all of it. Bukowski's poetry was Bukowski's judgment of the world and his place in it.

FV: Do you think Bukowski's writing persona was a fake?

AM: No. I've read a lot of his prose and poetry, which I know you have, too, Fred. *Everything he ever was* is in them. It's enlarged, perhaps, and painted with more literary colors, but, all in all, Charles "Hank" Bukowski was authentic. He never lost his roots, his need to remind us how he felt about the suburban dreams and hopes, the luckless guy or gal who he felt compassion for, the absurdity of how life can be wasted. He caught love and gentleness in his writing, as well as the harsher side. And he saw humor, dark humor, in just about everything.

ANN
MENEBROKER

BUK

From *The Habit of Wishing*, with Rosemary Cappello and Joan
Smith (Goldermood Press, 1977, USA) the following is Joan
Jobe Smith's favorite Ann Menebroker poem:

THE BULL THAT DIED IN THE RAIN
Poem by Ann Menebroker

He came to me in a dream
holding a light
and beckoning.
Because I dreamed, there was
no danger, and I followed.

He showed me an eternity
of dreamers
masturbating on death, whose
desires were finished.

In the night of my learning
there came a hunger. When I woke,
the dream was slowing digesting

and the plenty of my being
began to eat the bed.

FV: What is your favorite poem that you have written?

AM: My poems scare the hell out of me because I'm not sure how they get on the page. I don't have favorites. I have a brief love affair with the newest one I've finished. No loyalty at all!

FV: Which is your favorite poem written by Bukowski?

AM: One of my all-time favorites is "beans & garlic." But there were many others.

FV: Bukowski's face has been described as "beastlike," "Neanderthal." Recently I read a critic's description of Bukowski's face as "a bowl of walnuts." What did you see in Bukowski's face when you first saw him in person?

AM: I saw all the poems of his I'd ever read. I saw his voice. I saw the man.

FV: You've been a longtime friend of the American grit-poet/musician legend Kell Robertson and even published some letters with him, *Mailbox Boogie,* via Zerx Press, in 1991. How did that come about?

AM: Kell was introduced to me by our mutual friend, poet/editor, Ben Hiatt, over the telephone sometime in the mid- or late-1970s. You've heard of "phone sex"? This was phone friendship. Since then, Kell and I have kept up a prolific correspondence, we talk on the phone, and I've met him in San Francisco, Sacramento, Folsom, California, and Santa Fe, New Mexico. I don't remember whose brainstorm the idea for *Mailbox Boogie* was, and it doesn't matter. We asked each other questions through the mails, put those letters in a book and added some photos and poems. Mark Weber at Zerx in Albuquerque, New Mexico, published it. It's a pretty wild, uneven book, and that can be blamed on me, because I edited the letters. And there are typos and a few other errors in it. Kell and I have an enduring relationship. In 1990, he asked me, "What is this odd rapport we seem to have?" A decade later, I still can't answer.

Ann Menebroker by Henry Denander

It's there. It continues to work, and "if it ain't broke, don't fix it." Kell now makes his home in Santa Fe, New Mexico, where he writes, sings, drinks warm beer, and howls with the coyotes.

FV: Who or What, at this stage of your long, amazing life, is the real Ann Menebroker?

AM: I'm not finished yet. I'm just coming to another crossroads section. I've done a lot of failing (in attempts at things) and a little succeeding. I look like a retired librarian. I feel like that wild woman, off and on.

If Bukowski suddenly appeared at your door there at your home in Sacramento, California, alive and kicking, what would you say to him?

AM: "Don't Try." [Epigram on Bukowski's gravestone.]

UPDATE: As of 2012, Ann Menebroker resides in Sacramento, California—her work totaling twenty-five poetry collections, including *The Treasure of Small Gratitudes* and *Interludes of Passion* (Kamini Press, Sweden, 2012). Corresponding since 1974, Ann Menebroker and Joan Jobe Smith have possibly produced enough epistolary poet-pal pages to surpass four volumes of Victor Hugo's *Les Misérables*.

I TURN TO BONE AND OTHER STONES

Poem by Ann Menebroker
Sometimes when I am
with the lean dogs
the poems come, not because
I have expected them
or needed them, not because
I am clever or literary,
but because the light of the room
turns to bone
and the mad animals are famished.
What should be remembered is,
it takes very little to live, or die,
or love, and less
to write a poem.
What I call poetry
you may call my escape, but surely
whatever it is
leads us all to the same absurdity
for which none of us
can be blamed.

(Previously published in *Three Drums for the Lady,* **Second Coming Press, 1972, USA.)**

From cover of *Bukowski Review Three*

(drawing by David Hernandez)

"I feel gypped by dunces as if reality were the property of little men with luck and a head start." **CHARLES BUKOWSKI**

FRANCEYE

Interview by Fred Voss

francEyE and Fred Voss first met in April 1994 at the Buk-owski wake at Arundel's Bookstore on Melrose. This interview was conducted via e-mail September 2000, with francEyE responding from her home in Ocean Park, California:

FV: Fred Voss: What have you been up to lately, francEyE?

FE: For the past month or so, I have been following a practice of William Stafford's and of the Irish Bards, writing first thing in the morning lying on my back. I've never done this before, and so far I like the results. I've been retired from my day job for over ten years now, living alone in an apartment that was brand new when I moved into it and whose rent is subsidized by HUD, so that I have avoided the fate I always expected of dying homeless on the streets. It's still hard to get used to this way of life. Recently, though, I tried to envision moving to another community so that I could be nearer my daughter—my rent subsidy is "portable"—but I found that I could not possibly imagine living anywhere but here in Ocean Park and still being myself. Although an atheist, I go to church every Sunday, to a little neighborhood church full of activists and radicals. We celebrate the pagan holidays—the vernal and autumnal equi-noxes, summer and winter solstices, and the "cross-quarter days" that come between the four corners of the year—with rituals on the beach where we sing and talk about the seasons of the year and the seasons of our lives. As I write, the most recent one was Samhain—the Celtic holiday that falls near Hallowe'en. The word means "summer's end" because the Celts recognized only two seasons, summer and winter, which like Beltane occurs when the veil be-tween the two worlds, of the living and of the dead, is the thinnest. Last summer, I read—in the food section of the *Los Angeles Times*— a wonderful account by Vincent Schiavelli of summer in Sicily, and learned in Sicily that August is considered the first day of winter.

This is because the harvests beginning then provide the food that will be preserved to be eaten when the earth is barren through the cold time. I thought a lot about how I could take something from the summer to get me through the dark, and I began to think too about what I had brought to the winter of my years from my own high summer, painful as it was, that is sustaining me now as I deal with loneliness, pain, embarrassing leaky sphincters, and a couple of leaky heart valves, the deaths of peers, and in general the downside of being so old and wise. I'm very grateful to my younger self that I came to California, sought out Charles Bukowski, and gave birth to our wonderful daughter who now has herself given birth to a most magical person, Nikhil Henry Bukowski Sahoo. Nikhil was four years old on July 23, 2001. I'm still going to poetry workshops—another gift from my "summer"—and to poetry readings, which were very rare back then, wonderfully abundant now. Hardly anything in my experience compares for sheer pleasure to reading my poetry (or other people's poetry) aloud to an audience, and I have always had the wish to be able to recite at least some of my work from memory. Lately I have come up with a few poems that I can do that with, and I hope that I will have more.

FV: How did "francEyE" evolve from Frances Dean Smith?

FE: My friend Linda Princess Thomas, now of Montclair, New Jersey, gave me the name when we were both new on the job, doing clerical work in a gemology laboratory in Santa Monica. In order for the gemologists to work at their microscopes, the lab was in near darkness except for the lamps on our desks, and the atmosphere was rather depressing. Linda found ways to counteract the gloom. I'll never forget the day our boss told her, "Linda, you have to file the diamond reports now," and Linda said, "No, I don't have to. There's only one thing I have to do in this life and that's to die. About the rest I have a choice." Linda gave everyone nicknames, and one day she said to me "You're not plural, you're singular. From now on you're francEyE." Of course not everyone's new nickname stuck, but I embraced mine with glee. Since 1960 when I divorced my husband, Wray Smith, I had been inwardly without a name. Names were attached to me but they really belonged to my ex-husband or to my long-dead father, toward whom I was painfully ambivalent. I tried various pen names, but when I heard this one I knew that was it. The only question was how to spell it. That took a lot of discussion and the form I use now, "francEyE," appeared when the late *Caffeine* published a poem of mine, and the youngsters to whom Rob Cohen gave free rein to play with the type put it on the cover that way. I saw it and felt a start of recognition; the EyE seemed to make it clear how to pronounce it, and of course I liked the anti-conventional lack of a capital F. I also like that the spelling is not rigid. I can't write like Shakespeare, but I can have a shape-changing name like his.

FV: Which poets or writers have amazed you or influenced you as an artist the most?

FE: I'll never forget looking for the first time at *Carmina Archilochi*, translations by Guy Davenport of fragments of poems by the ancient Greek poet Archilochus. What a fantastic poet. I call him the ancient Greek Bukowski. *Carmina Archilochi* and Richard Wright's *Haiku: This Other World* are books I pick up almost daily. As I child, I adored Vachel Lindsay and wanted to emulate him and be a tramp, earning my supper with poetry. When I was older and reading Edna St. Vincent Millay, I was turned on to Countee Cullen by my swimming counselor, Lois Smith, who encouraged my poetry as well as my swimming. Later I came to revere Langston Hughes (whom Vachel Lindsay helped gain recognition). At about the same time, I discovered Thomas Gray's "Elegy in a Country Churchyard." Carl Sandburg never fails me, and his recent posthumous *Billy Sunday and Other Poems* made me very happy. Jimmy Carter is not a very accomplished poet, but some of the poems in his collection *Always a Reckoning*, especially "Rachel," reward rereading. I like to pair him with Jim Autry, whose *Nights Under a Tin Roof*, like Carter's poems, provide a window into a world I will never know first-hand. I have met some younger poets who continue in their tradition, portraying a white Southern boyhood without apologizing for it or trying to pretty it up. When people ask me who my favorite poet is I always say Sharon Olds and Charles Bukowski. As far as I am concerned, neither one of them ever wrote a bad line. Both of them write in free verse, but it is not the form that I adore, it is the willingness to hew to their own personal truth at whatever cost to bourgeois ideas of taste or manners. Quincy Troupe is another of my heroes, as is Steve Kowit—and then really their name is legion: Scott Wannberg, Jerry Quickley, Wanda Coleman, Michelle T Clinton, Fred Voss, Gerry Locklin, oh and of course Billy Collins and Ron Koertge. These are just some of the people whose work really moves me and whom I would like to emulate. In November, I got to hear again a poet I hadn't heard or read for ten years ago, Doren Robbins. I have loved his "The Big Store" for years, and his new work continues to amaze and delight. There's a poet living in the Valley whom I just heard and read for the first time in the fall of 2000; she's about my age and her name is Florence Weinberger. I long to be able to write as movingly and honestly as she does, and I hope she will soon find a wider audience. Her book *Breathing Like a Jew* took my non-Jewish breath right away. And now I realize that I almost forgot the late William Pillin, and remembering him brings me to the great, great John Harris, Joseph Hansen of *One Foot in the Boat* and *Ghosts*, and of course big John Thomas. Michael Datcher. A.K. Toney. Pam Ward, Jimmy Santiago Baca. I can't stop. There's a novel by the Dutch novelist Maria Dermout, *The Ten Thousand Things*, that has had a lasting influence on me and that I reread more often than I do *Moby Dick*.

FV; I understand you've been a poet since your early years. How did your relationship with Charles Bukowski, during or after, affect your writing?

FE: Reading Bukowski confirmed for me some idea of what really matters in poetry that I had been groping toward with some trepidation; I suppose you could say that his writing gave me permission to try to write the way I had always believed one should. I don't think that my personal relationship with him affected my writing; it affected me in other ways.

FV: Which of your poems are your favorites?

FE: Of course, whatever I have written most recently is always my favorite. If I look beyond that I can identify certain landmarks, certain moments when I finally broke through in a poem on some theme that I then would not have to wrestle with any more, or found myself able to do something I had not previously been able to do. "Yesterday's Song" is such a poem. It is the first one I wrote that I am able to remember without looking at the page. It was also thrilling to me because poet, artist, and bookmaker Barbara Maloutas illustrated it and made a book of it that I could give to my grandson Nikhil, then three years old. His mother said she had to read it over and over to him; he couldn't get enough of it. (Poem featured on pages 175 and 176.)

FV: Which of Bukowski's poems is your favorite?

FE: If I'm reading Bukowski, my favorite is whichever poem I am reading right now. Most recently that was "Escape," from the posthumous collection *Betting on the Muse*. Probably my all-time favorite is "Poem for Personnel Managers" from *The Days Run Away Like Wild Horses Over the Hills*. This is a long prosy poem that many people don't like, but I go back to it again and again, and it is the one I always recommend to people who know Bukowski only from his prose. Another that stays with me always like a mantra is "the priest and the matador" from *It Catches My Heart in Its Hands*.

FV: Do you think Bukowski's writing persona was a fake? In other words, how much of Henry Chinaski was "real"?

FE: No, of course his persona wasn't a fake. It was a persona, a mask; we all have them. Writing, I think, is a lifelong process of removing masks. There is no end to them.

If Bukowski suddenly appeared at your door, alive and kicking, what would you say to him?

FE: How should I know? I don't even know what I'm going to say when I answer the telephone until I say it. The image that comes to mind when I confront the question is of giving him a big hug.

POST SCRIPT: Frances Dean Smith (francEyE), mother of Marina Bukowski Zavala, grandmother of Nikhil Henry Bukowski Sahoo and Clara Marie Bukowski Zavala, died June 1, 2009, weeks after S.A. Griffin produced her poetry collection *Last Call*.

POEMS BY FRANCEYE

JUST BROWSING

There you are on the cover 25 years younger with your hair slicked back

and your tiny, shapely hands that used to stroke our shoulders

They stroked Jane's shoulders that are under the ground now

 and Barbara's shoulders and her neck that wouldn't turn,

 and they stroked my shoulders and Liza's

 and Cupcakes's and all the Lindas's

while you told magical stories to put us to sleep—

the world's handsomest man, with scars,

masquerading as Mr. Ugly—

and all I want to do is kiss you and stay with you forever.

francEyE

Amber Spider

(Cover Art by Marilyn Johnson)

In 2003, Pearl Limited Editions published francEyE's exquisite collection *Amber Spider.* "Sturdily, over the years, francEyE's become a Southern California treasure. Wearied by a world that hasn't worn her spirit down, francEyE's poetry reflects some of the finest that can come from a woman with a wise heart. If we women could return to our moonborn roots and sit again in the hut or cave, I would like to sit close enough to francEyE for our shoulders to touch or at least be allowed in the first row to watch her work her immortal magic..." JOAN JOBE SMITH

Forget I have tiny pig eyes and like to go to workshops

and never sweep the floor.

Forget you called me a whore,

puked in the bushes,

always passed out and had to be dragged to bed.

Oh you sweetheart, there on the jacket, thank you for kicking me out,

and for these magical stories to put me to sleep.

CONVERSATION AT ONE LIFE

Are you a senior citizen?

Nope.

Not yet, huh?

Maybe not ever. I kind of like just being old.

HERMAN

said history

will pass you by if you

don't take part in it. I'm waiting

to see.

UNTITLED

My sweat

as I take off

my shirt today—a whiff

of someone hot yesterday by

the fence.

A beard
on a woman
makes a boy laugh out loud,
and she can laugh at him, who's still
beardless.

YESTERDAY'S SONG

I'm walking up the hill.
I'm walking up the hill.
I'm walking up the hill;
 it's hard,
 it's hard.
I'm walking up the hill
I'm walking down the hill
to the top.

I'm dancing on the hill.
I'm dancing on the hill.
I'm dancing on the hill;
 it's high,
 it's high.

I'm dancing on the hill,
on the top.

I'm looking to the bay.
I'm looking to the bay.
I'm looking to the bay;
 it's far,
 it's far.

I'm looking to the bay
down there

I'm walking down the hill
I'm walking down the hill
I'm walking down the hill
to the beach,
to the beach.
I'm walking down the hill
pretty fast.
I'll dig myself a hole.
I'll dig myself a hole
I'll dig myself a hole

in the sand,
in the sand.
I'll dig myself a hole.
Good-bye!

francEyE and Fred Voss (2000).

(Woodcut by Loren Kantor)

*"Perhaps tomorrow my nose will be longer:
new shoes, less rain, more poems."*

CHARLES BUKOWSKI, **"Beerbottle"**

A BEAUTIFUL LIE

Essay by Fred Voss

I AM READING BUKOWSKI'S *HAM ON RYE* FOR THE FIRST TIME IN TWENTY YEARS. I haven't been reading Bukowski's posthumous editions of poetry. Only occasionally in the past few years have I read some poems from Bukowski's old books. I've been letting the man who inspired me to become a writer at rest, getting a little perspective on him. He's been dead over ten years now, and I wonder as I begin *Ham on Rye:* Will Bukowski still hold up?

Will he compare with Hemingway, Flaubert, Dostoevsky, Shakespeare, Raymond Carver, all those great writers I've been reading lately?

The first thing I notice is his lack of style, compared to Hemingway and Flaubert and the rest. It's like he's just talking to me, like he's hardly a writer at all. Maybe the American critics are right; maybe he's not to be compared to the greats. Maybe he's not even really a first-rate writer.

But then, before too long at all, I feel Bukowski' s presence, and the magic begins all over again. I realize I've missed Buk. I've missed his plain, just-another-guy-stepped-off-a-factory-line-job-and-talking-to-me-over-a-beer lack of pretense, lack of artifice.

In *Ham on Rye,* writing about being a student in fifth grade, Bukowski describes writing a paper for the teacher about going to see President Herbert Hoover in L.A. Because Bukowski's father made him stay home to mow the grass, Bukowski couldn't go to see President Hoover. So, Buk made up a grand essay about how he had seen President Hoover cruising through a stadium full of people in a car and how a plane had written about prosperity in the sky, how the sun had come out the moment President Hoover stood up in the car to acknowledge the people, how even God seemed to be there for the president's big day. The teacher loved the essay, causing

Bukowski to observe, "So, that's what they wanted: lies. Beautiful lies. That's what they needed. People were fools."

And then I realize it's not that Bukowski doesn't have a style, it's that his style has finally fulfilled the dream of Wordsworth and Whitman to write literature in the language of the common man. His style is in not having a literary style, neither the high style of Shakespeare nor the terse macho style of Hemingway or the minimalist craftsmanship of Flaubert or Carver. With Buk, the style is in the emotion, in the power of what he has to say, the anger, the humor, the insight, unfiltered by any self-conscious literary style.

Yet, Bukowski manages to soar, manages to grip me with a completely authentic, direct magic, a magic woven of his life and his fierce independent being. And suddenly I am grateful all over again. Grateful someone is speaking to me, grateful someone is offering himself to me directly, without any games or pretenses, on a deep and intimate and honest level.

HONEST.

In *Ham on Rye*, Bukowski is telling me the truth, speaking the truth to me, plainly, powerfully, from life, from *his* life, *his* life as he lived it and no one else could live it. He is giving his life to me, along with all his great intelligence and compassion and courage, with no "beautiful lies" to get in the way.

Style doesn't get any better.

"Buk, One Line," Illustration by Henry Denander

"What the hell, we'll all wind up link sausage on cracked china."

CHARLES BUKOWSKI

(Illustration by Billy Jones)

"...dying is sometimes not so much going somewhere as it is apologizing for leaving the rest of the bastards behind."

CHARLES BUKOWSKI, *Wormwood Review:22* (1966)

ELEGY FOR A GIANT

Essay by Fred Voss

First, I discovered Bukowski in the university library, and it was magic—nights up smoking cheap cigars and drinking cheap booze getting gloriously drunk and enlightened with Bukowski all night, reading everything, *the Erections, Ejaculations, Exhibitions and General Tales of Ordinary Madness*, the *Crucifix in a Deathhand*, all the poetry and prose and that picture of him hanging onto that boxcar ladder...

It was magic and it changed me and I was never the same and though I went to graduate school for a year I quickly dropped out and found myself filling up a boardinghouse room and then a dive apartment in Long Beach with the smell of chain smoking and beer drinking and on-the-edge-of-suicide survival working busboy and factory jobs and knowing it was worth it, knowing it was right as I read *Burning in Water Drowning in Flame* and *The Days Run Away Like Wild Horses Over the Hills*, and something he'd given me made me burn inside as I suffered and made it on not even knowing that I would be a writer, just that I was doing what I had to do and that it was right, days

and nights of steel dust and furnaces and a burned-up mattress and tears in my beer listening to Hank Williams and no woman for years like Bukowski at the start of *Women* still I held on with nothing but his poems and some kind of crazy stubborn will to go on

and I did go on

Bukowski

leading me through suicide madness and bikers

and women who threw me down into the hard asphalt of their rejection

without my own poem, without my own voice, I had

Bukowski

somehow leading me out of the darkness and toward the light

of finally finding my own voice and my own poetry

which I owe to him

as much as maybe my life

and much more and so

you see

that for me a great great light has gone out of this world

Yet

I look at my bookshelf 30 Bukowski books wide and realize that

light can only really get brighter

and brighter

and that I will have it

always

You must have plenty of sea-room to tell the truth in.

HERMAN MELVILLE

BUKOWSKI BOULEVARD

Poem by Joan Jobe Smith

For years before Bukowski died, just
to feel Bukowski's vibes, Fred and I'd
drive across the Vincent Thomas Bridge
To San Pedro to Santa Cruz Street we
named Bukowski Boulevard where Bukowski
lived in a big house with blue awnings
we'd drive by again and again and on
the way we'd say what would happen this
time; this time Bukowski'd be standing
on his sidewalk and he'd wave at us
and yell, "Fred Voss. Joan Jobe Smith
I've bene waiting for you. Come on in.
I've got your favorite beer, Fred, and
 Joan, some pouilley-fuissé for you"
and we'd go into Bukowski's big house
where Bukowski'd offer us his softest
chairs, he'd tells us his secrets, why
he REALLY wrote poetry, he'd show us
his limited editions and when Fred
admired "Crucifix in a Death Hand,"
Buk'd say, "Take it, kid, it's yours
Yeh, I know Red Skodolsky's priced it
at two-thou, but it's yours, Fred, for
I've always admired your work. And for
you, Joan, here's an ode, an apologia
for all the times I've insulted you."
Then he'd lead us to his dining room
for the feast he'd prepared just for us:
Peking duck, prime rib roast au jus,
chocolate chip ice cream and then on
our way home, Fred and I'd say, "Man,
that Bukowski, he's gotten soft. From
now on we're hangin' with Micheline."
but since Bukowski died, we hardly
ever drive by his house anymore, and
when we do, it's hardly any fun at all

NOTES OF A DIRTY OLD MAN

Poem by Joan Jobe Smith

My kids didn't like it when Bukowski
called me late at night, sometimes on
school nights, walking them up. Mom!
one of them would yell up to my bedroom.
it's that dirty old man again, none of them
old enough or well-read enough to know
then about his writings called "Notes of a
Dirty Old Man," them calling him
that because of seeing him at the
party I gave in his honor, watched
him pretend to piss into an empty wine
bottle. Why does that dirty old man
call you all the time? they asked me.
Why do you talk to that dirty old man?
they asked me. Bukowski was hard to
explain to them, especially hard was
explaining to them how fascinating he
was, even when he was drunk, blathering
on, not knowing most nights he called
who I was, sometimes calling me Linda
or Jane, one night saying, Hell, all
you women are either named Linda or
Jane or Smith. It wasn't until my son
took English 1A in college and saw the
Taylor Hackford film on Bukowski that
at least one of my kids understood, or
at least almost understood Bukowski.
Wow, Mom, my son said, Bukowski's famous.
My teacher said he's a genius. And Bukowski
was right here in our house. He sat in that
chair. But then my son remembered the
wine bottle. But, Mom, why, if he was such
a genius and was so famous, why did
Bukowski have to be such a dirty old man?

DUSTING BUKOWSKI'S HEAD

Poem by Joan Jobe Smith

Eight weeks since my husband bought the
head of Bukowski, a bronze life-size
masterpiece, and for weeks we had to
put up with all those puns and "head" jokes
the same sex joke in 1970 between Bukowski
and the sculptress that brought them
together for years, the original head they'd
fight over for custody like a love child.
Eight weeks since Bukowski's bronze head
came to live in our living room on the
coffee table amongst our personal debris
and Bukowski books and you should see
how amazing it is how sunlight or candlelight
adheres to Bukowski's bronze head and makes
his hair glow as if perspiring alive or
pomaded with electricity and you should
listen to the cool quietude of this piece
of art-man and how it makes you imagine
you hear him ha-ha-ing among the trumpets,
eight weeks and I go to dust the bronze
head of Bukowski, the wooden base white
with dust but when I do there's not one
speck of dust on the dust cloth or the
bronze head of Bukowski. I swear.

EGGS OVER EASY

Poem by Joan Jobe Smith

I was frying eggs over easy when
I heard Bukowski had died and
suddenly the yolks came alive,
grew to the size of heavyweight
Golden Gloves smashing my spatula
and jaw awhile the kitchen swelled
shut around me like a big, blackened
eye. Bukowski's obit was in the Thursday
newspaper, my favorite paper of the
week for the Food Section, the recipes
(this week sickening ones of what to
do with peanuts), the supermarket ads
(this week St. Pat's Day specials,
corned beef for 89 cents a pound,
cabbage for nine, rye $1.69 he'll
never eat again, if he ever did,
or the wine I later drink with my
husband who mourns more than me
as he listens to a Bukowski Live tape
and reads over and over the only letter
Hank ever wrote him. Hank never knew
was too busy to care, that his life
changed ours, that we'd come to know
his mojo poetry as well as the backs
of our hearts where manna and mortality
are stored. We'd wanted him to
live to be 400, after all, he was 200
at age 30, he was supposed to keep telling
it like it is forever, be our Poet Man,
nexus and code breaker of nether worlds.
But no one dies when you want
him or her to, death seldom an Ides
of March or hemlock time for which

you can set your alarm clock as, as he
was quoted in his obit: You carry in
one hand a bundle of darkness that
accumulates each day. The eggs
over easy were the coldest I ever ate,
a March ninth wind blowing in through
the window turning them to ice).

   –   **March 9, 1994**

"I arrive on time in the blazing midday of mourning."
CHARLES BUKOWSKI

I once said to Bukowski, "You've got small hands," when he held mine briefly, look-
ing at a ring I was wearing—and he said, "You've got big feet!" As we looked down
at my feet—size 5—I said, "Yeh, Buk, my feet are huge." Joan Jobe Smith

CHARLES BUKOWSKI: AN INCH-WIDE 24-KARAT GOLD-LIPPED COGNAC GOBLET IN THE HUNTINGTON BOTANICAL GARDENS

Essay by Joan Jobe Smith

"WHO WOULD'VE THOUGHT –" I OVERHEARD MANY SAY, most of them fans, September 20, 2006, at the Charles Bukowski Induction "Celebrating Bukowski" at The Huntington, in San Marino, California"—"that some day Charles Bukowski's archives would be housed *here*?" *Here* being one of the most magnificent, elegant libraries with some of the most exquisitely designed classic architecture, most fabulous art exhibits and gorgeous botanical gardens in the world.

Unthinkable, unpredictable, incongruous, many thought that night that a man who often never shaved, habitually bet on racehorses, usually wore loose plaid shirts or T-shirts seldom tucked into his baggy nearly worn-out corduroy pants or jeans, and drank copious amounts of alcohol every day, a "Philosopher of Ugly," "Outsider" poet/writer whose phenomenally prolific words were often criticized as vulgar and coarse, that this strange, non-conforming complexity of a human being would be honored with adoring, near-hagiographical accolades similar to those assigned to a Walt Whitman or a Carl Sandburg and provided a literary nook as exclusive, welcoming and respectable as provided William Shakespeare.

Know who would've thought it? At least one time that I know of (and undoubtedly inestimable times I didn't know of): Charles Bukowski Himself thought it. And said it out loud—after I said what I said to him, August 16, 1976:

...good human beings save the world
so that bastards like me can keep creating art,
become immortal.
if you read this after I am dead
it means I made it.

CHARLES BUKOWSKI

"People Look Like Flowers at Last."

"Someday, Bukowski, you'll be the greatest poet in the world."

And Bukowski said: "Baby, I'm already the greatest poet in the world."

It was the wee small hours of his fifty-sixth birthday and he was full of himself—and drunk, but not too drunk to be in total control of his own thoughts which were seldom obscured with neurotic self-doubt or lack of confidence.

August 16, 1976 was when I told Bukowski I'd nicknamed him "Epic Glottis" and made him laugh—which wasn't hard to do. Bukowski had one of the quickest wits, widest smiles, and easiest laughs I'd ever known, seen, or heard. Bukowski was also alone that birthday. He'd telephoned long distance to ask me to drive to Hollywood where he lived, thirty-five miles away from where I lived in suburbia. He wanted me to party with him—at one o'clock in the morning. He had a case of beer. Beer made me sick, I said. He also had two bottles of Port. I drank Chianti, but preferred Dom Perignon champagne.

"Hell, I can't afford Dom Perignon, kid. I'm just a poor poet."

"Where's Cupcakes?" I asked. He'd professed countless times to me in 1976 that he was madly in love with the young, voluptuous, red-haired beauty. He bragged about having written a Black Sparrow book of love poems, *Scarlet*, to her, priced at a hundred dollars each.

"Gone. Cupcakes's not at home. She's left me, just like Linda did," he said.

He lied; I was sure of it. Bukowski always lied to me about his Women. After all, he was an Epic Glottis, his brain a swirling cerebral universe that filled his frothing throat with fabulous starry-night tales of extraordinary madness. Not to mention ejaculatory exclamations. I suspected he only asked me to come over to make the sweet Cupcakes jealous, trying to set up a scene, create potential for a cat fight between two women as he'd tried many times with me against his old girlfriend Linda King who'd left him for good last December (1975). I never went alone to his Carlton Way flat nor any other Bukowski abode. I dared not to.

"How's Pearl?" Bukowski asked. "When's the male chauvinist pig issue coming out?"

I didn't have any money to produce it, I told him. I'd spent all my student loan money on law school tuition and books. But I had hopes for an NEA grant I'd applied for and told him I might get issue #4 out by Christmas. In 1974, I'd met Anaïs Nin who said she would write a piece for it. Anaïs Nin always had a lot to say about macho men.

"Oh, yeah? Anaïs Nin? All right—" Bukowski pro-nounced Anaïs "anus"—of course—instead of "ahna-ees."

I told him I'd just yes-terday talked to her on the telephone. In two years of friendship, Anaïs Nin and I had logged by then about four hours of long distance chat—she, in Silverlake, calling me, forty miles away in Orange County suburbia. Anaïs and I have a lot in common, I told Bukowski. Poetry. Her middle name is Joan. She loves to dance and thinks it fascinating that I was a go-go girl for seven years.

"Oh, yeah?" Bukowski muttered, almost interested in what I was babbling.

Yeah, Anaïs wants me to teach her how to go-go dance like the girls on TV. And Anaïs wants me to drive her up to Big Sur to meet Henry Miller when she's feeling better. A year ago she was diagnosed with cancer. And the chemotherapy has made her sick—but when she gets used to it, she'll get well, she said.

"Cancer. That's bad shit. Henry Miller, huh? He's a good writer."

Anaïs Nin, 1970s, Silverlake (Los Angeles), California

Many critics back then had compared Bukowski's writings—mostly the profanity, surrealistic parataxis and self-referential streams of consciousness—to Henry Miller.

"Henry Miller's one of my favorite writers," said Bukowski. "But I'm a better writer," he clarified.

Anaïs thinks Miller will like me, I told Bukowski. Anaïs says maybe he'll want to write something for the *Pearl* #4 male chauvinist pig issue.

"Miller's a lech, baby. Be careful. Ahh, but you're too old for him!" Bukowski laughed. (Miller was eighty-six in 1976.)

At nineteen and a half years my senior, Bukowski had been saying I was too old for him since he'd met Cupcakes, who was thirty-one years younger than Bukowski. I was almost old enough to be Cupcakes' mother. But it didn't matter to me how young his Women were.

Nothing Bukowski said could make me feel worse than I already felt that long hot summer of Bicentennial 1976. Law school had made me feel rotten: a crucifix in a death hand; surreal: I had no south of no north; oxymoronic: I burned in water, drowned in fire while the days ran away like wild horses over the hills.

"You're getting fa-a-a-at, Joan Smith," Bukowski'd said to me the previous month when I'd visited him at his Carlton Way flat with Marilyn Johnson.

Bukowski was always insulting me. Why would I ever want to drive thirty-five miles at one o'clock in the morning to visit Charles Bukowski, fifty-sixth birthday or not? Not even if he offered a magnum of Dom Perignon. And he didn't.

And thirty years later, in 2006, which, had he lived, would've been his eighty-sixth year, that long ago Beer Can in the Garden as he once called himself in 1976, would magnificently morph to become an inch-wide twenty-four-karat gold-lipped crystal cognac goblet in The Huntington Botanical Garden when it was announced September 20, 2006 that in 2010, Charles Bukowski would be inducted into the hallowed Literary Valhalla at The Huntington.

Four years seemed like an impossible wait on September 20, 2006, as family (Linda Lee Bukowski and Marina Bukowski Zavala with her mother francEyE—Frances Dean Smith) and fans of Charles Bukowski gathered gaily in the chandeliered little theatre not to bury Bukowski but to praise his Huntington Library Worthiness: the legendary John Martin, Bukowski's long-time benefactor, friend, and Black Sparrow publisher; The Huntington Library Director David Zeidberg; Bukowski Curator Sue Hodson; "Love, Bukowski" Producer Joanne Gordon; and Bukowski poetry performers and readers that included actor Harry Dean Stanton and poets Neeli Cherkovski and S.A. Griffin. Linda Lee Beighle Bukowski, pretty in a bright red designer suit, resembling perhaps a gift-giving petite great-great granddaughter of Santa Claus, was formally thanked by David Zeidberg for donating a portion of her late husband Charles Bukowski's priceless archives to The Huntington. As she raised her arms into the air and waved exuberantly, she received a cheering, standing ovation from a very enthusiastic and grateful audience of nearly two hundred.

The Huntington, a rarefied spot of green Eden, with its magnificent monolithic architecture reminiscent of The Parthenon, luxuriates regally in San Marino, ten miles north of downtown Los Angeles, California, upon a parcel of land of equal aristocratic measure as Versailles, Windsor Castle, and the Taj Mahal. Oil Tycoon Huntington, the founding King who also named after himself Huntington Park, twenty miles to the west, and Huntington Beach—sixty miles southwest where Bukowski read many times at the Golden Bear nightclub in the 1970s down the Pacific Coast Highway, south of thousands of billion-dollar oil wells mostly pumped dry by then. Until the 1960s orange groves sprawled all around The Huntington horizon, one wide orange-and-green-leafed shoulder leaning as far as Riverside, California, a hundred miles southeast. Oil and oranges—commodities that made the tony neighborhood tonier as the decades ran away like wild horses past the city of Pasadena and then over the Verdugo Hills and San Gabriel Mountains to the north.

The same fans who attended the 2006 induction, and more, showed up there that warm ninety-degree October 27, 2010, evening to see the opening ceremony celebration, "Bukowski Aloud." (But francEyE—Frances Dean Smith—mother of Marina Bukowski did not live to see this; she passed away June 1, 2009.) I met some of the loggers-on to Bukowski.net, viz, the moderator Michael Phillips. Met Neeli Cherkovski for the first time, though I'd known of him and read his writings for thirty years; and Roni Braun, coordinator of the proposed Charles Bukowski Museum in Buk's birthplace, Andernach, Germany, who also publishes the Germany-based Bukowski Society Newsletter.

Way up high, waving from the little theatre rooftop at all of us down below and at the baking ultramarine California autumn sky, flapped a huge flag the size of two boxcars, a Goliathan loincloth, perhaps, bearing the age-sixty-something face of Charles Bukowski posed with a lit cigarette between his manicured fingers, smoke rings halos over his head, his eyes intensely wise looking right through You.

"Who would've thought this would happen?" Someone questioned again the Great Gods of Literature. I did not reveal the Final Answer: "Bukowski Himself."

My machinist poet husband Fred Voss wore—one of the few times ever—his black T-shirt with the word "Bukowski" sprawled across Fred's muscular chest at the top of a Bukowski portrait, then below it the words, "Dog From Hell." A-list Dignitary, generous Donor of her late husband's priceless literary works, Linda Bukowski, accompanied by the 2004 *Born Into This* documentary producer John Dullaghan, winced when she saw Fred's T-shirt. Then, frowning at

Joan Jobe Smith at the Huntington Library Celebration, October 27, 2010.

him, she remarked that the T-shirt's Bukowski image had been produced without her permission. It was an awkward moment at an event expected to be as fun and lighthearted as the 2006 induction ceremony. Fred emitted a distressed sigh, tired from the long drive in rush-hour traffic, and my feet hurt from the half-mile walk in high heel thong sandals from the parking lot to this little theatre—but I joked anyway:

"We're innocent, Linda! Honest, we are! I'll give you the address of the art store where we bought the T-shirt back in 1999 so you can call the poetry police and press charges for plagiarizing and bootlegging Bukowski's image and words."

I laughed all alone at my own joke and shot a picture of Linda Bukowski, Generous Benefactor dressed in brown and John Dullaghan all spiffed up in wool apparel suitable for a foggy day in London own rather than this dusty-hot heat-wave-plagued upper Los Angeles County.

"SMILE Linda and John!" I called to them, then: "One-two-three and –" CLICK and double-flash, atomic-blasted my clunky, crappy camera, blinding both of them, the backlash through the viewfinder stunning my vision, too.

When Linda Bukowski nearly tumbled, in a sort of state of shock, to the ground, I said, officious intermeddling paparazzi, meaning it: "I'm so sorry,"

Then I bent down, patted her dainty, trembling shoulder, maternally, to soothe her because Bukowski had made a big deal how much older I was than her, too. And quickly Linda Bukowski got over the plagiarized T-shirt controversy and the camera's sudden atomic blast, and moved on with her Good Life to procure a glass of open-bar wine.

Linda Bukowski and John Dullaghan, director of the Charles
Bukowski documentary *Born Into This*, at The Huntington,
San Marino, California (October 2010).

John Dullaghan, barely acknowledging that he knew Fred and me, giving us both limp gratuitous but anonymous handshakes, had video-taped Fred and me twice in the 1990s, about four hours' worth, in our condo in Long Beach—Dullaghan a newbie filmmaker back then shooting footage for his proposed documentary. But Dullaghan wound up dumping Fred and me and all the stuff we babbled and bragged till past midnight in 1999, me proud to've known Bukowski, Fred glad to be one of Bukowski's most adoring fans who owned nearly all of Buk's books that included the valuable *Crucifix in a Death Hand* plus a bronze repro sculpture he bought for fifteen hundred dollars in 1996, that in 1972 Linda King designed of Bukowski's head. Dumped, we were; Outtakes so's to make room for Buk-loving celebrities Bono and Sean Penn. Can't blame him.

Happy hour waning, twilight gone, a group strolled away toward the dark gardens to look at the Bukowski exhibit in Friends Hall, titled "Bukowski Out Loud." Fred and I tagged along behind Marina Bukow-ski Savala and her son, Bukowski's grandson, Nikhil Henry Bukowski Sahoo. Marina's baby daughter, Clara Marie Bukowski Zavala, born September 26, 2008, had stayed at home. Nikhil, fourteen years old, wore a crisp white dress shirt tucked into neat, dress pants. When Nikhil smiled he looked just like his mother Marina who looked just like her father Henry Charles Bukowski.

If I hadn't known Charles Bukowski, I would not have recognized him as his widow Linda Bukowski chose to represent him at this long-awaited exhibit. She'd totally created, with curator Sue Hodson's expertise, a brand-spanking-new and magnificent silk shantung purse out of the infamous dirty old man's porcine ear. Who would've thought that Bukowski could be spruced up like this?

In each portrait, shot by some of the finest photographers he'd met in the 1980s, he'd been rehabbed, transformed into a New Man of Letters—and possible male model for a *Gentleman's Quarterly* cover, a distinguished, haberdasher sartorial cross between Humphrey Bogart and T.S. Eliot. This Poet Man exhibited here dared to eat a peach, care and not to care. If this Charles Bukowski had've sipped Dom Perignon with you, he would've said, "Here's looking at you, kid." And when you walked into a piano bar, he would've always requested "As Time Goes By."

The finest Danish butter wouldn't've melted in this Poet Man's mouth, let alone the lard drips from a cheap *carnita* bought from a *taqueria* on Skid Row. This suave designer-suited poet had hair that glowed from overhead museum lights making halos over his sparkling head that used to shine because it needed a good washing. This Poet Man would not have let his shirts fall off their wire hangers onto the pile of dirty underwear amongst empty beer cans and wine bottles on the closet floor of his Carlton Way flat; nor would that Poet Man have left dishes in the kitchen sink dishwater for a week until euglena floated on top of the stagnant water inside the filthy coffee cups—and sure bet there would not be whisker snips in such abundance in his bathroom sink and on his sticky bathroom floor that they resembled a million armies of black ants at a toothpaste-plop picnic. All that disarray, borderline squalor I'd seen in 1976 in his Carlton Way apartment, I obviously only imagined.

I remembered one of Anaïs Nin's famous quotes: "We don't see things as *they* are. We see things as *we* are."

There was no mention or memorabilia or exhibition of Bukowski's Women—except the Book *Women* he wrote, tucked, like an apostrophe in the corner of one of the superlative proper-noun displays of Bukowski's Other, Saner Achievements. No big deal made of the long-ago hardworking artful editors who'd helped make him famous: Marvin Malone of *Wormwood Review* who'd featured him in countless issues from the late 1960s until months after Bukowski's 1994 death and Malone's demise in 1996. Where was the tribute to

In 1987, Black Sparrow Press published Bukowski's screenplay for *Barfly*. The book's cover photo featured Faye Dunaway, Charles Bukowski, and Mickey Rourke.

Gypsy Lou and John Webb—the artists who'd printed at their own great expense in the late 50s-mid-60s *The Outsider* and immortalized Bukowski with their exquisite handmade, hand-bound production of *Crucifix in a Death Hand*?

Most prominently exhibited were a few insignificant, ordinary love notes he'd written to Linda Lee, his wife, his Last Linda, editor John Martin's Black-Sparrow-produced Bukowski books, posters of the films made of his books, namely Cannes Film Festival-feted *Barfly* with the oft-seen promo photo-shoot of Buk with Faye Dunaway and Mickey Rourke. And other things of precedence and personal importance to Linda Bukowski that quickly slipped my mind as I tried to recollect them while I walked behind Marina, Nikhil, Linda Bukowski, and John Dullaghan on the way back to the little theatre to watch the new celebratory Buk Show about to play there.

But maybe I got distracted because my feet hurt so much. Got hung up on my own self and couldn't see the Garden for the flowers and green leaves Linda Bukowski had meticulously arranged. Perhaps Linda Bukowski was also an Anaïs Nin fan and took to heart one of Anaïs's other famous quotes: "How wrong it is for a woman to expect the man to build what she wants, rather than to create it herself."

Linda Bukowski, indeed, had Done It Her Way. Wouldn't you?

But I had seen, clearly, and most wonderful of all: the green inter-twining love displayed by the gentle mother Marina whispering to her beloved son Nikhil, wide-eyed, both of them, as they pointed at and gazed upon the Art (sans Women) and artifacts of the Great Man, Father, Grandfather they loved and missed so much, displayed with care, posed just so, beneath the glossy glass cases.

"Are you going to be a poet, too, Nikhil?" I asked Bukowski's handsome grandson, resisting the urge to pat his thick black hair like I do with my own black-haired grandson Nathaniel. Nikhil, only fourteen years old, was very grownup looking, already sporting a patch of fine moustache meanderings above his Bukowskian thick lips and beneath his Germanic Bukowskian nose. Nikhil looked up at his mother Marina who smiled at me and shrugged her shoulders.

Nikhil Henry Bukowski Sahoo, October 2010.

"Who knows? Maybe," Marina replied for her son, who seemed a bit shy.

I did not remind her that in 2004 I'd published in *Bukowski Review3* Nikhil's very first poem he written when he was age five—permission and copy of the poem provided to me by Nikhil's maternal grandmother, Frances Dean Smith (francEyE).

U   UR   RUU?

RUU? UR   UR

URUR   ur

URU   RU?UR ur

UR   RUU? ur

For poet Fred Voss and me, the best part of the "Bukowski Aloud" Program was hearing Nikhil read his grandfather's poem "Fuzz," one of our favorites—about three small boys with toy guns pretending to arrest him for being drunk on his way to buy whisky at a liquor store. And the surprising standout: Marina's heartfelt and deeply touching talk—one of her first public appearances: "Hank, My Miraculous Father" describing her father, how much she loved him, he loved her, and how much she misses him and always will.

After Bukowski's and my Long Night together, August 16, 1976, spending the night together yet thirty-five miles apart, him in bed in Hollywood, me in bed in suburbia, talking on the telephone till dawn's early light, I only saw him two more times— the penultimate, in September, 1976, at his encore performance at the Troubadour. After Bukowski's brilliant, hilarious and well-received performance, I asked him to autograph my copy of *Factotum* I'd bought from him via mail, paid for it with a check he cashed, and I used the cancelled check for a bookmark.

As Bukowski and I chatted while he signed *Factotum* (which he'd nicknamed "Racktotum" in a letter to me), I stood next to Linda Lee Beighle, a petite, fragile, and attractive young woman who was meeting him for the first time in person. Soon she'd be wooed by Bukowski after Cupcakes and Linda King—his First Linda—leave him. His Last Linda and he'd have a stormy relationship for years till they finally marry in 1985.

Though I never saw Bukowski in person again after Autumn 1976—the last time at his Bodega Bar reading in Long Beach—he continued to telephone me now and then, complain to me of his new, *younger* women I would never meet. When he and the Last Linda broke up, briefly, in 1978, he asked me to go to Germany with him on a reading tour. A set up, I was sure of it—to insult me somehow; also, he'd let me know, the cad, I was his third choice. But soon he and Last Linda reconciled and she got to put up with his shenanigans—controversial and triumphant—on the road in Europe that photographer Michael Montfort captured on film for Bukowski's 1979 *Shakespeare Never Did This,* and later, in 2012, re-produced and translated into French by France's 13eNote: *Shakespeare N'a Jamais Fait Ca* with a foreword written by Gerald Locklin, Fred Voss's poem "Bukowski's Groupie" along with an excerpt of my memoir "Charles Bukowski: A Beer Can in the Garden" (*Une Canette de Biere Dans le Jardin*).

Then, out of nowhere, after three years of silence, Bukowski sent me on July 3, 1981, a submission to *Pearl* adorned with his exuberant cartoons—his trademark sunbursts, birds, dogs, flowers, self-portrait of the little man smoking a cigarette and holding a bottle with the label "x." Warm, line sketches, always witty, sometimes gritty, or gruesome might be described as a cross between James Thurber and a drunken monkey. Three poems he sent me, too: "the new woman," "the poets and the foreman," and "i am a reasonable man" (about his last love tryst with his First Linda, Linda King).

"My guess would be that if *Pearl* exists," he wrote in longhand, "it's a matter of how you feel when you get up in the morning. If *Pearl* hasn't folded, enclosed may still be returned and both of us will still get up in the morning. Yeah, Hank." He added his new telephone number, now unlisted, at his new, big house on a hill in San Pedro he'd bought with his nouveau riches—the house, not the hill. So I telephoned him, the first time ever I'd telephoned him:

Yes, I said, I did feel like doing *Pearl* when I got up in the morning but I just never had the money to do it because I never got that National Endowment to the Arts grant. Bukowski, sober, glad to hear from me, drank good white wine as I forlornly complained that *Pearl* was defunct; there'd never be that Male Chauvinist Pig issue with him as feature along with Anaïs Nin and possibly Henry Miller. [But in 1986, after Marilyn Johnson buys her first p.c., she'll help me reprise and fund *Pearl*. And in 2012 we'll celebrate the forty-sixth issue—and twenty-six years of continuous publication.]

Then on July 15, 1981, Bukowski wrote me again: a friendly three-page letter handwritten in his inimitable, bold, black-ink-confident, artful-script: "Just off living with a fairly good girl for three years. But she wanted 'soul-expansion' so I let her go. I am not one to compete with the eternal wonders of the universe…am working on being immortal…"

When I telephoned again, the second time I ever called him, he was still sober, in a good mood, still drinking good white wine— Liebfraumilch that day.

"I've changed, kid. Cleaned up my act. I'm rich now, kid. I'm the richest poet in the world. Richer than Rod McKuen. Don't have to do any more goddamned readings to make money. Got rich off my poetry and bought this big house and just drink the good stuff now that doesn't make you crazy like that cheap stuff. Got into the good stuff on my 1978 German tour. You should'a seen me over there, kid. They're crazy about me in Germany. Sold fifty thousand copies of my book that Weisner published in Germany, *Poems Written Before Jumping Out of an 8 Story Window*."

Five years from then, when he's sixty-six in 1986, Bukowski's bibliography will include thirty-two books of poetry, five books of short stories, and four novels. What I've always loved best about him and his work, his ceaseless, epic poetry and prose depictions of Women and his undying love and lust for them, will surpass Balzac, Baudelaire, Toulouse Lautrec, Tennessee Williams, and possibly even Hugh Hefner's bountiful perpetuation of femme-inspired artifact and become a heaped-high virtual-virtuoso Mt. Everest— inarguably the most words ever written about women by one man.

"Come see me, kid. Come do a Greek dance with me. I'll buy you that magnum of Dom Perignon you always wanted."

How could I resist that? A magnum of Dom Perignon. Okay, I said. He and the younger woman, whose name he never mentioned, had broken up for good—he assured me of this.

"She's gone. For good," Bukowski promised me.

"I do not want to be a point on another one of your crazy Love Triangles ever again," I told him.

"Kid, now when did I ever do that?" Bukowski asked, innocently, the finest Danish butter unable to melt in his cool mouth.

"You used me to make Linda King jealous, and Cupcakes, too."

"Aw, kid, that was the Old Bukowski. This is the New Bukowski, working on being immortal. I've changed. I'm rich, kid. I can buy you a magnum of Don Perignon."

So for the first time, ever, I said Yes, I'd come see Charles Bukowski—the New Bukowski—who lived in a big house on the San Pedro hill. I asked if I could bring one of his fans, Marilyn Johnson's daughter, Margot, a freshman at University of California Irvine, a teen girl prodigy who'd just won the *Seventeen* magazine's short story competition. Bukowski liked the dark-haired, attractive Marilyn the times he'd met her and flirted with her.

"Margot would like to write a paper about you for one of her lit classes."

"Sure, bring her over," said Bukowski, "I dig teenaged prodigies."

The day Margot and I planned to visit Bukowski, our Buk Books packed up to have him autograph, I telephoned Charles Bukowski— my third time ever I'd ever called him. I needed directions to his house up on the San Pedro hill where I'd never been before.

"HELL-OH! WHO THE HELL IS THIS AND WHAT DO YOU WANT?" A Woman answered Bukowski's telephone—a furious, ferocious Woman, a Wild Woman, drunk, or tortured by Karma, dangling in the tournefortia, possibly by her thumbs.

I asked for Charles Bukowski.

"HANK!" the Woman screamed beerspit from some balcony. "IT'S FOR YOU, YOU SON OF A BITCH! IT'S A FUCKING WOMAN!"

"YEAH? WHAT DO YOU WANT?" Charles Bukowski, the alleged NEW Bukowski, roared into the telephone receiver. "WHO THE FUCK IS THIS?" Bukowski snarled.

Bukowski was drunk. He'd never talked mean and loud like this to me before. A Raging Bull and Godzilla were mere mockingbirds wishing you good luck compared to this Bukowski, this shit-faced raving maniac Bukowski I'd only heard tell about from Linda King, only seen in Taylor Hackford's 1972 PBS documentary *Bukowski*.

"Joan Jobe Smith," I said.

"WHO?" Bukowski said in a normal voice, though the Wild Woman in the background continued screaming at the top of her lungs, angrily, painfully. Maybe his drunkenness had caused him memory loss—probably after he drank that magnum of Dom Perignon he'd promised to buy for me. And, of course, my name was a common name. Joan Smith, one in a jillion. Maybe the Jobe part confused him.

"Joan Smith," I abbreviated, using less syllables to make it easier for him.

"OHHHH—JO-OHHH—JJJOANNNN—SSSMITHHHH," Bukowski pretended to ponder. Then said, smugly, snarling, a cross between W.C. Fields and the Big, Bad Wolf: "OH YEAH—JOAN SMITH. I remember you now—yeah—JOAN SMITH—Linda King's **OLD** girlfriend."

And then Bukowski hung up the telephone receiver—a very noisy clang like a bowling ball in an iron bathtub. So. Har-har-har. After all those years of being sort of nice to me, Bukowski had set me up again. Made me one of the pointed parts of another of his crazy Love Triangles. The cad. Betting on his Muse. That same-ol' dirty old beer can in the garden.

"Cosmodemonic," Henry Miller might've called him.

"Brute," for sure Anaïs would've named him.

Now, here, today, after just publishing the forty-eighth issue of *Pearl* (with the genius expertise of my old friend and co-editor Marilyn Johnson), I am nearly the same age as Anaïs Nin when I met her in 1974. I slouch and simmer in a Septuagenarian Stew, March 9, 2012, eighteen years after Charles Bukowski's death to leukemia, while I recall and write and conclude all the above and below about that dirty old beer can in the garden Bukowski I first knew in 1972—when gasoline cost forty-cents a gallon—versus the 2010 unrecognizable inch-wide, twenty-four-karat gold-lipped crystal cognac goblet in The Huntington Botanical Gardens Bukowski when gas cost four dollars a gallon—and I finally think of a writer who best captured the "charismatic," complicated character of Henry Charles Bukowski and Bukowski's Cognac Goblet/ Beer-canniness, his holy-hellacious devil or angel love dog from hell or

puppy love madman or mensch burning in watery oxymoronic am-
bivalent-paradoxical didacticism: that Epic-Glottis Buk armed with
alliterative gerund grenades and hardcore hyperbole, an eternally
embedded war correspondent in the insane, bombastic Battle of the
Sexes: Robert Louis Stevenson's *Dr. Jekyll and Mr. Hyde.*

So. Though the last time I'd actually see in person Charles Bukowski was October, 1976, when he read at the Bodega, a bar on
Second Street in Long Beach, California, a lonely womanless guy
that night—Cupcakes saying her Goodbye-forevers, Linda King, his
First Linda, gone for good—Bukowski, after stumbling onto the
small, dark stage, knocking over the microphone, forlornly inform-
ing the packed-house of rabid fans who'd crowded into the small
bar to see him read his poetry: "What you see here is the results of a
weeklong drinking binge"—the last time I'd ever "see" Charles
Bukowski would be in my imagination, September 1981: snippet
images of his pissed-off snarling mouth, his drunken eyes sunken
beneath a furrowed brow as dark as a back alley awning in Skid
Row, socking it to me in his *comme habitude, fait accompli, coup de
guerre,* personal style. What a Cosmodemonic lover man. What
a character.

Then I receive word from a poet pal about the American poet
William Wantling, novelist, ex-Korean War Marine, ex-convict and
college professor from Peoria, Ohio, citing a Wikipedia entry: "William Wantling died of heart failure brought on by weeks of exces-
sive drinking; believed to have been triggered by the brutal, abusive
behaviour of his idol Charles Bukowski [whom] he'd invited to a
poetry reading and Bukowski had acted like a tyrant, insulting everyone and saving his most disgusting behaviour for Wantling, calling him a worthless poet who had run out of things to say. Wantling was devastated by this and went on a weeks- long bender that
resulted in his fatal heart attack [May, 2, 1974 at the age of 32]." Oh,
Bukowski, I mutter out loud. You brute.

Looking for redemption, reacquaint myself with the finer Charles Bukowski I'd first fallen for in 1972 when I first read *The Days Run Away Like Wild Horses Over the Hills*, I reread the intelligent dissertation by the first Bukowski scholar to receive his Ph.D., Jules Smith, *Art, Survival and So Forth: The Poetry of Charles Bukowski* (Wrecking Ball Press, Hull, England 1997). On a poetry Facebook site, I scrolled through entries from California State University Long Beach MFA candidates discussing Bukowski, comparing him to Emerson, Philip Levine (for "worker aspect"), Whitman, Ginsberg, Marianne Moore, Tolkien, Hemingway, D.H. Lawrence. But the laughable entries of Justin Bieber and Bugs Bunny made me forgive Bukowski, think lovingly of him and his odd ways enough to look into the Buk Book I'd always liked best: *Love Is a Dog From Hell*.

Found my machinist-poet husband Fred Voss's copy that he'd bought in 1977 after he dropped out of the UCLA Ph.D. program in English Literature. Fred's Bukowski book all beat up now, dog-eared from many readings, stained in 1977 with coffee cup and beer can rings (not out of careless disrespect but on purpose, because Fred figured Bukowski would like it like that); on pages 190-191, a smudge from a spider Fred squashed in 1983; June 19,

In 1977, Black Sparrow Press published Charles Bukowski's poetry collection *Love Is a Dog from Hell*.

2011, the beat-up book classed up by an autograph: "For Fred Voss—Cupcakes" on the day I interviewed her.

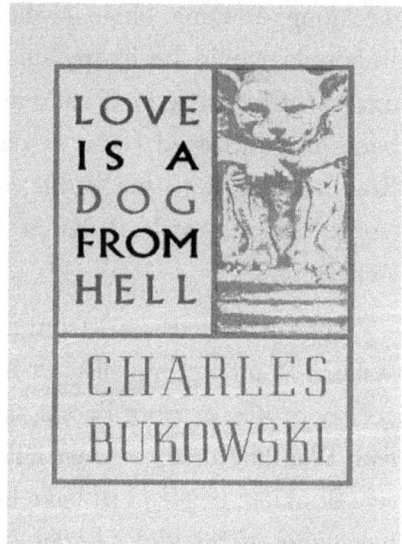

I went searching in that *Love Is a Dog From Hell,* as so many forlorn Bukowski lovers have, for wise words to lift me up from mundane and misery, find again the Great Poet and Woman Lover who'd always impressed me. On page 65, I met up again with Marina Bukowski's mother, Frances Dean Smith, in Buk's love poem to her, "one for old snaggle-tooth" ("...her hair is white...a body most women wish they had...she has created a better world,/she has won..."). On page 171, "red up and down" about Pamela Miller Wood (aka Cupcakes/Scarlet): "...people ...wondering where such an ugly/old man could get/such beauty./I didn't know either.." In another poem, Buk describes Cupcakes' hoop earrings similar to the ones she'd worn when I met her in 2011. Loving-and-hating poems about the First Linda, Linda King, are in this book, too, but one of my favorites is from *Pearl #3,* 1975, and *Das Ist Alles—Charles Bukowski Recollected,* 1994, *Pearl* Special Editions, "the big ride": "now I have...love like a bomb in an airport locker...she/has little green and/golden moths sewed /against the sides of/her..."

Those Women, Bukowski's Women—for me—represent the best of him and his writings. And, oh, how wrong were those uptight, wanting to do-right feminists back then in the 1970s. Fighting for the best equal rights for us male-dominated women via social change, I know—along with some requited revenge against male chauvinist pigs—many of the Women's Libbers back in the 1970s got stuck (no pun intended), as I often do, on Bukowski's prickling priapic poems and prose paragraphs and got put off and took off running and never looked back.

Until today. Now this current new generation of been-there, done-that, seen-it-all lit-loving world-weary women love Bukowski—his warts, acne vulgaris scars, dirty boxer shorts, beer cans in the garden, and all. And if Bukowski didn't love us Women back, pledge his troth till death do us part, he at least noticed us, listened loud and clear to us goddesses or nemeses, antagonists/ protagonists, epiphanies or ennui. Bukowski wrote tons about us good, bad, and snugly babes, broads, bimbos, barflies, barmaids, dolls, divorcees, single moms, strippers, streetwalkers, gold diggers, poets, Ph.D. profs, and broken-hearted babycakes, our warts, woes and all—and validated our hard-knocked existences.

But though Bukowski claimed in his lament poem, a wish poem for a Good Woman "quiet clean girls in gingham dresses..." "all I've ever known are pill freaks, alcoholics, whores, ex-prostitutes, madwomen...I need a good woman... more than I need this typewriter...Mozart...quiet, clean girls in gingham dresses.." Bukowski's Real Women—the ones he loved in real life—for me, once again—represent the best of and most marvelous of all the "literary" characters I've read about during my entire literature-loving life, and possibly as equally marvelous as Charles Bukowski Himself.

Then I remembered that Bukowski had called me one last time, years later: "Joan Smith!" he demanded, as sober, sane, serious as my recent student loan bill collector. (My ten-year-old student loan, plus interest, now totaled what a condo in Las Vegas would cost.)

Bukowski's earnest voice seemed apologetic, perhaps for our last unpleasant encounter, that 1981 phone fiasco. But no, he'd called to tell me he was getting married.

Congratulations, I said.

"You had your chance, kid. You lost the race."

I didn't know I was in the running, I said.

"You were a long shot. But I picked a winner. She's a good woman."

Good for you, I said.

"I'm still rich, kid, and getting richer."

I'm still impecunious, I said, had just quit my teaching job to care for my dying mother.

Paying no attention to my pathos, he said he'd written a screenplay, *Barfly*. Told me when the movie came out to look for a character, a female small press editor, based on his first wife Barbara Frye—and me, Joan Smith.

"But mainly I called to ask you not to call me anymore—or write me." (I hadn't called or written since 1981.) "My future wife is very possessive and I've vowed to be faithful."

Good luck, I said.

"Good luck to you, too, kid," he said, kindly—"au revoir and das ist alles," and hung up, gently.

(I later read the Barfly screenplay and found the description Bukowski had written about Tully, the character based on me and his first wife Barbara Frye: "TULLY in her late twenties. A class lady. She's over-educated, mod, warm, nervous, sad, kind. Very intelligent and understanding, she has a tendency to appear more joyous than she is. She has been unlucky in human relationships but persists in the search for another. Perhaps her weakness is that she is too well-meaning. She won't let go of it, it's almost a disease. And others don't want to get infected. At this point, through a family inheritance, she has financed a West-Coast-based magazine, The *Contemporary Review of Art and Literature*. Her life, like so many other lives, has been unlucky and still is.")

Joan Jobe Smith at the Tongue & Groove Bukowski Tribute, June 30, 2012.

I did write Buk one more time, in 1988, asking permission to print in my recently reprised *Pearl* his poem, "The Closing of the Topless and Bottomless Bars." But he didn't remember writing a poem with that title. Advised me to contact John Martin. But I didn't.

And then, on June 30, 2012, at Conrad Romo's Tongue & Groove Bukowski Tribute when I appeared with actors Harry Dean Stanton and Rebecca DeMornay and poets Gerald Locklin, Jack Grapes, Dan Fante, Wendy Rainey,

Kenneth "Sonny" Donato, Chiwan Choi, et al, at the sparkle-plenty Water Court surrounded by skyscrapers and city lights in downtown Los Angeles, I read my favorite Bukowski poem "The Closing of the Bottomless and Topless Bars" to an audience of three hundred plus, began with: "the idea that moral outrage only/can be felt by/the gifted and the noble and the/intelligent and/the sensitive and the/powerful/that is the biggest joke of/all..." and, mustering as much of a nasally Bukowski imitation as an ancient go-go girl can, I ended with Buk's punch line: "...I've just got to/believe those Supreme Court boys/don't care about anything real and just/can't get it up/anymore..." I got lots of laughs, too—just like Bukowski did back in the 1970s when I saw him read it twice—from memory.

I count myself lucky to have known most of his Women, personally: Those exceptionally, extraordinarily brave, loving, sometimes wild Women—who had to be brave, loving, *and* wild to survive him. Each Bukowski Woman a work of art. Each Bukowski Woman a fable—and each a Muse to bet on not just for Bukowski, but any man.

Should there ever be a Bukowski's Women Tour, as Pamela Miller Wood kidded about in her foreword to this book, I heartily volunteer to tag along—not as referee as Pam suggested, but as choreographer so's to have a chance to dance with them.

And if I'd ever had a chance to dance with them—all of them together a vaudeville of devils or angels without wings—a bone palace ballet—or one of them ask me to teach her to go-go or disco as Anaïs Nin once did, all of them dolled up—not in square-housewife housedress or square-dance gingham—but rather in white fringe bikinis and go-go boots or tight jeans and rhinestone Zappos or Manolos or Nikes or purple shantung caftans or feather boas and tiger skin mini skirts, barefoot contessas or black-leather'd dominatrixes or see-through white satin toga-clad Muses—

With Jane, Bukowski's ancient Love, his Clio, I'd dance a slow fox trot to Stevie Wonder's "I Just Called To Say I Love You."

With Bukowski's Euterpe, Muse of Lyric Poetry, his first Literary Love and Dedicatee, Annie Menebroker, I'd not dance but sit with her upon a plush velvet sofa and sip magnums of Dom Perignon and listen to Sinatra sing "I Got You Under My Skin," "That Old Black Magic," and "One for My Baby and One for the Road."

With silver-haired Earth Mother Frances Dean Smith, I'd dance a gentle jitterbug to Glenn Miller's "String of Pearls" because of all her francEyE-authored strings of pearl poetry she sent to *Pearl* we published the fifteen years I got to know and admire her.

With Linda King, Bukowski's First Linda, a combo Erato, Muse of Erotica, Thalia, Muse of Drama, and Terpsichore, Muse of Dance, I'd not dance but watch her land of a thousand dances, an autodidact soloist of her own vivacious drumbeat, bump and grind.

With the voluptuous scarlet-haired Pamela Miller Wood—Cupcakes, a Venus-Baby Doll de Milo—I'd dance the Bugaloo to Credence Clearwater's "Keep On Chooglin'" and disco to the Bee Gee's "Stayin' Alive"—chooglin' and stayin' alive what she's done with grand *elan vital* most of her life.

And with the willowy, lovely Last Linda—the Good Wife—a Callisto-Calliope, I'd want to dance that Greek dance Bukowski asked me many times to do. Because the stalwart, Do It Her Own Way Linda Bukowski surely, sure-footedly danced it many times and must know it by heart and soul—with a few tangos and twists and shouts thrown in of her own invention. And then, at long last, I'd like to choreograph a chorus line of us all and dance a Polka to the Beatles' "Ob-la-di-ob-la-da life goes on…"

Lala how the life goes on…

And on.

As always.

"Life's bad but not too much so. I figure if I kick off right now, I've already done ten times ten…this is a great house…many fights with women here, cars roaring out the driveway at sunrise…I love women, especially when they love me. Take it easy. Be careful, Joan, Hank Buk."—1981

Drawing by Joan Jobe Smith, August 16, 2012.

OH, HENRY

Poem by Joan Jobe Smith

Bukowski told me the reason he chose
Charles for his writer name instead of
Henry his real first name was because
He didn't think Henry a very writerly
name and I, a full-of-myself undergrad
said, But what about Henry James, Henry
Miller, Henrik Ibsen, O. Henry? And Charles
Bukowski laughed, letting me know he was
glad I wasn't the bimbo he thought I was, and
I laughed, glad he didn't think me a bimbo
and he laughed some more, harder, his eyes
twinkling, his teeth big and white as he let me
know it wasn't so much knowledge he had
but psychic insight and that he could see right
through me and I stopped laughing because it
was scarier than hell to be known so well.

JOAN JOBE SMITH, founding editor of *Pearl* and *Bukowski Review,* worked for seven years as a go-go dancer before receiving her B.A. from CSULB and MFA from UCI. A Pushcart Honoree, her award-winning work has appeared internationally in more than five hundred publications, including *Outlaw Bible, Ambit, Beat Scene, Wormwood Review,* and *Nerve Cowboy*—and she has published twenty collections, including *Jehovah Jukebox* (Event Horizon Press, US) and *The Pow Wow Cafe* (The Poetry Business, UK), finalist for the UK 1999 **Forward Prize**. In July 2012, with her husband, poet **Fred Voss**, she did her sixth reading tour of England (debuting at the 1991 **Aldeburgh Poetry Festival)**, featured at the **Humber Mouth Literature Festival** in Hull. In 2013, **World Parade Books** will release her memoir *Tales of an Ancient Go-Go Girl.*

FRED VOSS, a machinist for thirty-two years, has had three collections of poetry published by the U.K.'s Bloodaxe Books. He is regularly published in magazines such as *Poetry Review* (London), *Ambit* (London), *Rising* (London), *The Shop* (Ireland), *Atlanta Review* and *Pearl*, and has twice been the subject of programs about his poetry on National BBC Radio 4.

In 2008, he was featured at **The Ledbury Poetry Festival,** and in 2011 he and his wife, poet **Joan Jobe Smith**, were featured readers at the University of Pittsburgh, and in 2012 he appeared at **The Humber Mouth Literature Festival** (Hull, England). Voss's latest book, *Hammers and Hearts of the Gods* from Bloodaxe Books, was selected by the UK newspaper, *The Morning Star,* as one of the Top Seven Books for 2009. In 2011, he was featured poet in a hardbound limited edition of *Dwang* (London, England), and in 2013 World Parade Books will publish his first novel, *Making America Strong.* His latest collection, *Art that Roars* (a duo chapbook with poet Mark Weber), is available from Zerx Press.

www.ingramcontent.com/pod-product-compliance
Lightning Source LLC
Chambersburg PA
CBHW071336090426
42738CB00012B/2916